Freedom
to Be Yourself

Mastering the Inner Judge

Freedom
to Be Yourself
Mastering the Inner Judge

Avikal E. Costantino

BOOKS

Winchester, UK
Washington, USA

First published by O-Books, 2012
O-Books is an imprint of John Hunt Publishing Ltd., Laurel House, Station Approach,
Alresford, Hants, SO24 9JH, UK
office1@jhpbooks.net
www.johnhuntpublishing.com

For distributor details and how to order please visit the 'Ordering' section on our website.

ISBN: 978 1 78099 191 7

A CIP catalogue record for this book is available from the British Library.

Design: Stuart Davies

Printed and bound by CPI Group (UK) Ltd, Croydon, CR0 4YY

We operate a distinctive and ethical publishing philosophy in all
areas of our business, from our global network of authors to
production and worldwide distribution.

CONTENTS

The world is not a courtroom,
there is no judge, no jury, no plaintiff.
This is a caravan,
filled with eccentric beings
telling wondrous stories about God.
Saadi

The inner conflict

I wake up, and as my day starts, so too do my first sensations and thoughts. Next come my plans – things to do, intentions for the day. But something else comes too: a pressure I know only too well. It may come as a voice inside or a sensation in the solar plexus, or a pressure in my forehead or a familiar heaviness on my shoulders. Behind each of these responses, lies the question: 'Will I make it?' The pressure arises not only because of the number of things I need to do or from the feeling that there never seems to be enough time to do all of it, but mostly, from a vague, even unconscious feeling that to do it all will take effort. How have stress and pressure become such constant companions in my life? When did I start running, having no time for myself, feeling distant from people and preoccupied? When did that happen? Is this what life is all about? I feel uncertain, afraid of failure and, more than that, I expect and in fact take for granted a level of stress in merely getting through my day.

The pressure is instant and, without realizing it, I am 'in the dock' and have started to assess and judge myself. I am measuring my worth – as man, woman, husband or wife, father or mother, son or daughter, worker or boss... Pay enough attention to your inner voices and you'll notice that from the moment you wake up there is no respite from this feeling. There may be temporary relief when you have accomplished a task... but soon, the pressure returns.

Part 1

Recognizing the Presence of the Inner Judge

Chapter 1

The Beautiful Mask

From childhood on, one of the things we have learnt to do – and continue to refine, becoming real artists along the way – is 'to pretend'. Daily, we put on a beautiful mask (with more or less sophisticated variations) and with it we move through the world, hoping to be considered truly authentic or, at least, not to be exposed as a fraud. We use the mask to avoid facing our frustrations, our isolation and any lack of satisfaction. We use it to avoid the sudden opening of an abyss where nothing makes sense, and questions such as, 'What am I doing here? What is this life about?' resound in a space that is empty of answers. We use the mask to avoid dealing with an almost unbearable level of tension and stress. We have, however, found we can keep the stress under control with medicines, alcohol, television, hyper-activity or simply by losing ourselves in the feverish search for money, success and recognition. We have learnt to hide behind the mask with such skill that in the end we believe we are that mask.

We believe that the mask is essential to our survival and, moreover, that without it we would not be able to function in society. We continue then to support the pretensions the mask contains; we continue to refine the strategies that keep the mask active and functional.

What a huge effort it is! But then, we get so used to it that we end up believing that's the only way to survive.

But I'd like you to stop for a minute and ask, 'Am I here to survive or to live?'

What will this book do for you?

My main purpose in writing this book is to explain what holds that mask in place, why we are so attached to it, what its function is – personally and socially – and to explore whether we really need the mask. I also investigate what might happen if we took the mask off and, knowing that it can serve a purpose, we look at how to use the mask and, importantly, avoid being used by it. We will look, more specifically, at that part of the psyche called the inner judge (also known as the superego) that protects and keeps the mask in place.

The superego

The superego uses judgments, admonitions, punishments, rewards, evaluations, standards of behavior and moral values to create, sustain and re-create our self-image and a particular representation of reality, forcing us to live in an inner world, and in relationships that are based not on the connections and inter-actions of real individuals, but on images and masks.

Essence is the centre, that which is your nature, that which is God-given. Personality is the circumference, that which is cultivated by society: it is not God-given ... If you enter into a well-developed personality you will find these three things. First, a very thin positive layer – positive, but phoney. That is the layer which goes on pretending: that is the layer where all your masks are contained. Fritz Perls used to call that layer the 'Eric Berne layer'. [Eric Berne is the author of the book *Games People Play*]

It is where you play all kinds of games. You may be crying within, but on that layer you go on smiling. You may be full of rage, you may want to murder the other person, but you go on being sweet. And you say 'How good of you to come. I am so happy, so glad to see you.' Your faces show gladness; that is phoney ... Parents are in a hurry to give this layer to the child. They are in a hurry because they know the child has to exist as a member of a false society. It will be difficult for the child to survive without it; it functions as a lubricating agent. This is a very thin layer, skin-deep. Scratch anybody a little and suddenly you will find that the flowers have disappeared; and rage and hatred and all kinds of negative things are hidden behind it.

That is the second layer – negative but still false. The second layer is thicker than the first. The second layer is the layer where much work has to be done. That's where psychotherapies come in. And because there is a great negative layer behind the positive, you are always afraid to go in, because to go in means you will have to cross that ugly phenomenon, that dirty rubbish that you have gathered, year in and year out, your whole life. From where does the second layer come? The child is born as a pure centre, as innocence, with no duality. He is one. He is in the state of unio mystica: he does not yet know that he is separate from existence. He lives in unity; he has not known any separation, the ego has not arisen yet. But immediately the society starts working on the child. It says, 'Don't do this. This will not be acceptable to the society; repress it. Do this, because this is acceptable to the society and you will be respected, loved, appreciated.' So a duality is created in the child; on the circumference a duality arises. The first layer is the positive that you have to show to others, and the second layer is the negative that you have to hide within yourself ...

These two layers are our split. The first layer is positive and false, the second layer is negative and false. They are false because only the total can be real. The partial is always false, because the partial denies something, rejects something, and the existence of a denied part makes it false. Only in total acceptance does reality arise.

(Osho, *Unio Mystica*, Rajneesh Foundation, Pune, India, 1980, vol. 1, ch. 2)

This description, from the spiritual leader, Osho, succinctly captures the conditioning and the reasoning behind developing masks. It also points to a fundamental split that happens in most people and is, perhaps, the major reason for our inner conflict and suffering. It is the split from our spiritual foundations.

When we are identified with the mask, we miss in fact, in ourselves, the third and more fundamental place that is our core, our center, our essence. And by missing that, we live in a partial, lukewarm way geared to survival but devoid of the dangerous splendor of living. We become immersed and entangled in what I call 'the contract of mediocrity'.

How do we unmask?

It's not an easy thing to do. Start unmasking by telling yourself the truth. We resist telling ourselves the truth about ourselves. It's often the most difficult challenge we face. It is also the most important one we can attempt.

So, how can we begin telling the truth?

An essential step is to acknowledge that inside us exists a fundamental conflict: between control on one side, and freedom and love on the other. Because of the painful nature of this conflict, we have created ingenious ways to avoid becoming aware of it and of feeling it.

We live in an almost constant state of denial of this inner conflict, of its motivations and of its devastating effects on our daily life, both within ourselves and in our relationships with others and the world around us; we continue to pretend that things are fine, that our life is going well. Often, the reality is quite different.

If only...

If only... we could stop for a moment to listen to the incessant inner dialogue that, more and more frequently, becomes a battle-field of opposite and antagonistic points of view, drives, commands and needs.

If only... we could stop for a moment and feel the effects of these battles in our body: tensions, contractions, psychosomatization of anger, fear, guilt, shame or the shadows of unfulfilled sexuality.

If only... we could stop for a moment and ask ourselves what we gain by keeping this constant weight of pressure caused by self-judgment, comparison, criticism.

If only... we could stop for a moment and listen to the gentle voice of our soul, we could easily observe that it is almost impossible to hear it, dominated as it is by the loud, aggressive and manipulative voice of our inner judge.

If only... we could notice that we never allow ourselves to be exactly as we are. Instead there is a constant pressure of how we 'should' be. It might be that we ought to be slimmer, richer, smarter, happier, stronger, more independent, more beautiful, more, more, more... and less aggressive, less indecisive, less needy, less greedy, less preoccupied, less, less, less...

If only... we would notice that every moment, every hour, every day, we live in an internal and external environment that is sending us a fundamental message: 'You are not OK as you are, you must be different. Once you've achieved this (smartness, independence, perfect weight, wealth...), maybe then, you'll be acceptable to yourself and others and you may deserve to be loved and respected.'

What is the effect of the judged life?

The inner judge invariably generates inner conflict and yet denies its existence; it survives on the creation of external conflicts.

Getting angry at someone else, taking revenge, gossiping, putting people down and humiliating them (often in very refined and indirect ways) allows us, for a moment, to discharge our energy and experience a brief relief and, often, a fleeting sense of superiority.

By externalizing the inner conflict we allow ourselves to

unload substantial quantities of energy that could, if repressed for a long time, damage us irreversibly.

Why do we behave in this way? We do this to survive. It is one of the clever and unconscious ways we regulate the charge and discharge of mental, physical and emotional energy, in our nervous system.

But it is also a habit that allows us not to assume responsibility for our life and to continue to blame others for what we are and what we do. Finding a scapegoat, someone to attack or criticize, someone to complain about, allows us to shift our attention from inside to outside and focus on resolving external problems instead of looking inside ourselves and dealing with the war that takes place inside us.

We avoid feeling our fundamental wound, which is the fact that we don't really know or recognize our worth; we are not in touch with our intrinsic value. We make our value dependent on the approval and acceptance of others or, at times, the domination of others.

We live behind the mask because we have lost the connection with our soul, have forgotten who we really are; forgotten that we exist as unique manifestations of Universal Creativity, of God, of the Absolute, of the Primordial Energy – whichever name you want to give it.

As we stubbornly hang on to this mask – called personality – we refuse to hear, to see and feel with our heart that voice inside us that wants us to be true and authentic. Instead we walk through the world surrounded by a cloud of paranoia, fear and competitiveness; isolated, unsatisfied and ready to attack others or to run away and hide.

Inquiry, meditations and visualizations

Throughout the book, at the end of each chapter, you will find a section called 'Inquiry, meditations and visualizations' in which I provide topics to explore that are directly related to the chapter and particular aspects of your relationship with the superego.

Inquiry – a brief description

Inquiry is not simply analysis, nor is it restricted to the field of logical deduction. On the contrary, inquiry that is really effective will continually bring us into contact with the unknown and challenge everything we think we know. Inquiry is dynamic and, if practiced with passion and love, can take us outside our 'comfort zone' opening territories way beyond our expectations and leading us to profound and immediate understandings that would not be possible using linear logic.

There are five simple steps to inquiry:

1. Formulate a question about your inquiry that gives a general direction of where you want to go.
2. Tell the 'story' – what you already know about that subject.
3. Widen your attention and notice the effect that this recounting has on you in the present – the sensations in your body, emotions and images as they appear in your consciousness.
4. Observe if the superego is active, if it attacks you, if there are judgments or symptoms of inner conflict.
5. Don't draw quick conclusions. Activate your curiosity and continue to question what is happening; why you have certain symptoms, how they relate to certain emotions, what lies behind a particular defense, what the superego's judgments remind you of? Maintain the contact with the thread while it unravels even if it appears fragmented.

The pillars of inquiry

The practice of inquiry is premised on four essential pillars.

Intention

To begin, we must truly want to know the truth; have the

'intention' to see, hear and experience the truth. It is revealed only if we are willing to tell ourselves the painful, unexpected, hard-to-handle truth; a truth that may be contrary to everything we have always thought.

Intention is a sword that helps us to separate what is false and what isn't, allowing us to recognize falsehoods for what they are. Fundamentally, however, intention does something else: it consciously reconnects us with our soul and its yearning to know itself by connecting us with a fundamental drive – curiosity.

Openness

A second essential element is 'openness' – to what we encounter while practicing inquiry. We will, invariably, find things we are not aware of, that we have hidden and tried to avoid by repressing them in our unconscious. Usually we come into contact with our superego, its judgments and prejudices, our structures of defense, the usual mechanisms through which we sustain our personality, our inner images and the ways in which we try to control ourselves and our relationships.

Being open means being willing to accept what happens in each moment. To tell the truth as it is: I am angry, I am afraid, I would like to run away, I feel blocked, I don't know what to do, I'm in a state of shock, I feel lost, I am closed... An awareness without choice or judgment, a direct and simple reflection of our experience, without trying to manipulate, glamorize, make palatable or acceptable. Openness also includes being aware of the tendency to judge and compare, and to see what effect such judgment has on us and on others.

Acknowledging not-knowing

The third pillar is 'acknowledging not-knowing' – being aware that all our knowledge is the result of events of the past and we cannot automatically apply that knowledge to the present. Certainly, that knowledge helps us read what is happening to us, but it can also act as an obstacle to our ability to answer in a creative and original way to events that happen 'here and now'.

This conscious attitude of 'not knowing' allows us a freedom from the superego; our attachment to our own personal story begins to dissolve. The baggage of the past becomes lighter, little by little.

Staying in the body

The fourth pillar is 'staying in the body'. We experience ourselves and our 'conditioning' not as an idea or a concept but, first and foremost, as a body. It is our body and our senses that are the doors of our perception; without them, how would we exist?

Conditioning means judgments, opinions, values, beliefs, prejudices that exist at a psychological and emotional level, but also at a physical level – a web of tensions, contractions, blocks, sensitivity, chronic postures and somatic illnesses. When we recognize our physical symptoms, as well as the emotional loads associated with judgments that are linked to the superego's attacks, we can unify our consciousness: our physical, mental and emotional bodies, and accurately identify the pattern of a particular behavior.

I deal with inquiry in far greater detail in Appendix A. I recommend that you read the Appendix before you begin the inquiry exercises.

In addition to using the pillars of inquiry, it is recommended you also use meditations, visualizations and writing.

- Meditations and visualizations: I will give you meditations and visualizations and, sometimes, body exercises to help take you more deeply into the material covered in the chapter.
- Writing: I recommend that as soon as you begin your exploration, you begin taking notes – in a diary or exercise

book – of the things, thoughts, feelings, ideas that come to the surface.

Inquiry

Let's start with the exploration of particular subjects that can help bring to the surface unconscious parts of your personal history, and to illuminate the behaviors which cause you pain and conflict. The exploration will also help you to become more intimate with yourself and the functioning of your personality, and to recognize your potential and specific abilities.

Notice if it's easy for you to do this exploration or if it causes you anxiety and resistance. Take 15–20 minutes for this inquiry, and if you have done it verbally with a partner, take another 10 minutes at the end to write down the main things you have noticed.

1. Explore the image of yourself that you like to show others. How do you want others to see you? What impression do you want to give? What are the qualities, facets, traits that you want others to value in you? How do you effort to present that particular 'face'? This means exploring what Osho has called 'the positive layer'. Are you aware of hiding a second layer where the negative images of yourself are contained? Are you afraid of being discovered?

2. Observe how you feel while exploring your outward image. What sensations do you feel in your body at this very moment? Are you at ease and relaxed? Do you feel any tension?

   Feel your breath flow in and out of your chest. Is there any constriction, heaviness, pressure? Does this image convince you or do you feel that there's something that's not right? Can you say where the 'not right bit' is? Observe if, and where, this image becomes a mask behind which you hide, and what it is that you don't want others to see.

3. Explore your reactions to rejection.

What are your reactions when you feel that the image you show others is not accepted, appreciated, when you are not noticed or understood? Observe the reactions in the body, where you close down, collapse, tighten, or 'disappear' and where you create a wall... and so on.

4. Explore the theme of self-value.

Observe where and how in your life your worth is defined in relation to the responses of others, and how and where a sense of intrinsic value exists, independent of the outside. Be as precise as possible.

Chapter 2

What Is the Inner Judge?

What is this presence inside us of which we are aware, sometimes vaguely and sometimes intensely, and that we call the 'inner judge'?

Sigmund Freud gave a name to this judge – he labeled it the superego, a name that clearly expresses its role. The judge is above the ego, much higher than the ego, and the 'super' part of the name evokes images of control and domination, images of parents standing over their child, images of the triangle, the triumvirate (in religious mythology) with the eye of God over all, scrutinizing and judging sinners on earth.

Sandra Maitri, a teacher of the personality system emphasizing psychological motivations known as 'Enneagram' (which identifies nine fundamental personality types), writes:

> As Freud's name for it in the original German – the Über-Ich – implies, its function is to oversee the Ich, our sense of 'I.' It preserves the status quo of the personality through its injunctions and admonitions, telling us what to do and how to be, what is all right within ourselves and what isn't. It evaluates our experience into good and bad, right and wrong, okay and not okay, and so on.
>
> (Sandra Maitri, *The Spiritual Dimension of the Enneagram*, Tarcher & Putnam, New York, 2000, p. 37)

But where does the superego come from? How is it formed? And, perhaps most importantly, why do we have one? What is the purpose of an inner judge?

Origin and formation of the superego

During the first years of its life, an infant is completely dependent on its parents. Foremost its mother and second, its father.

The mother has an irreplaceable role, providing nourishment and helping regulate the energy levels of her baby, intervening when the baby's system cannot adjust itself spontaneously.

When a baby is eating or suckling, for example, the mother has to intervene and help it free itself of indigestible things, or help release the air blocked in its stomach. The mother has to clean her baby of its feces and dry the baby when it wets itself, rock it to sleep and reassure it.

But above all, the mother is the person who creates the atmosphere of the environment where the baby lives. The way she cradles and takes care of the baby, the way she touches and hugs the child to her breast, leaves an indelible mark on the psyche and on the body of the baby.

The mother's presence, and the quality of this presence (or, conversely, her absence), her emotionality, her physical health, all generate significant variations in the so-called 'holding environment' for every baby.

A. H. Almaas is a meticulous scholar of childhood development and its effects on the formation of the personality and the consequent ability of individuals to show their individuality and potential. He originated the 'Diamond Approach', and writes:

> ... the holding environment is the environment during the first year or so of life, the period in infancy before the child begins to develop a separate sense of self. Initially, the environment is the womb; later on it is the arms held you, mother's lap, perhaps father and other people, the environment of your crib, your bedroom, your house – the whole situation. So 'holding environment' here means the totality of the surroundings and the general feel of it through the formative years. Mother is central to this

environment but it isn't limited to her.

(A. H. Almaas, *Facets of Unity*, Diamond Books, Berkeley CA, USA, 1998, p. 384)

The baby responds in a direct and immediate way (non-conceptual) to the changes in the holding environment and to the physical, psychic and emotional conditions of the mother.

According to Almaas,

> If the environment is a good holding environment, it makes you feel taken care of, protected, understood, loved, and held in such a way that your consciousness – which in the beginning is unformed, fluid, and changeable – can grow spontaneously and naturally on its own. The soul in this respect is like a seedling. A seedling needs a particular holding environment in order to develop into a tree: the right soil, enough water, the right nutrients, the right amount of light and shade. If it doesn't have the proper holding environment, it won't grow steadily and healthily. And it might not grow at all.
>
> (Ibid, p. 39)

We see then how harmony and the substantial emotional continuity of the holding environment is essential for non-traumatic growth and development of the baby.

The most important thing to note is that any lack of continuity or harmony in the holding environment immediately reflects as a danger to the baby's survival. Any negative emotional load on the part of the mother – a lack of warmth, of touch, attention; an angry voice, a cold look, a disgusted or distant demeanor – all of these are interpreted by the baby as a threat to its survival. The fear of dying is not psychological or emotional, but rather an experience in the body at a cellular and energetic level.

Later, the baby begins to have a sense of itself as a separate being, and its perception of external objects and therefore its ability to be self-reflective (based on the capacity to distinguish between subject and object) allows the baby to start to associate specific behaviors with variations in the quantity of love and care that it receives.

For example, there could be an association created in the baby between excessive crying and a response of detachment and impatience in the mother, or one in which the control of feces is gratified by smiles and tenderness, or where not screaming is associated with a calm and reassuring tone of voice, and screaming is associated with an impatient and cutting mother, and so on.

Some behaviors begin to stand out as painful and 'negative' – they involve a reduction or withdrawal of affection. Others are considered 'positive' as they are rewarded with certain amounts of love, care and affection.

The natural tendency of the baby towards survival and development will lead it to look for ways to re-establish a sense of harmony and balance in the holding environment through reactions that allow it to remedy the affective disorder. Almaas asserts again:

> If the holding isn't there or isn't dependable, the child will try to manipulate herself, her parents, and/or the environment to bring it about. The child might develop all kinds of ways to please the parents by doing things for them, entertaining them, or hiding her needs. On the other hand, she might try to distract them from their problems, throw tantrums to get attention, or become manipulative or even deceitful to try to get the holding to return ... The less holding there is in the environment, the more the child's development will be based on this reactivity, which is essentially an attempt to deal with an undependable environment.
>
> (Ibid, pp. 43–44)

A necessary condition to the functioning of strategies of reaction aimed at re-establishing continuity in the holding environment is the repression, in the unconscious, of behaviors judged 'unacceptable' by the parents or other authority figures in the family environment.

The behaviors, impulses, undesirable ideas and actions initially will be rejected and suppressed and, later on, repressed. Once they are repressed, they are no longer available to our consciousness.

Suppression is not painless

This process of suppressing or rejecting feelings is not painless. Effectively, the child is compelled to reject and hide some parts of themselves and of their behavior even before they are capable of experimenting with them, and of knowing and understanding them in a personal way.

The child has to accept and to succumb – on the basis of convictions, prejudices and external values imposed by the parents – or risk punishment, humiliation and isolation.

A pattern that could fit almost every family has to do with sexuality. Every child is naturally sexual and innocently curious and if they are supported and guided consciously, they can grow, discovering their sexuality in an unproblematic way.

From their earliest days, all children have to deal with fears, prejudices, taboos, conventions related to sexuality. They deal with moral and religious judgments, perversions and deviations, lies and silences of the parents and the wider environment in which they grow. Indoctrination and conditioning take the place of discovery and understanding.

What choice then does the child have if not to accept the indoctrination in order to survive, even before having the chance to develop their own idea about themselves and their experience? And, to hide from themselves and others the inner conflict between instinct and control?

With these conditions the child will develop an internal coercive mechanism that represents the imposed values and keeps control. This ensures that the unacceptable behaviors remain in the unconscious and the acceptable ones are actualized and expressed in order to receive the attention and recognition that each child so deeply craves.

Your parents told you, 'You are wrong, this is not right, this should never be done,' and a thousand and one times they repeated it. And you gathered one message: that you are not accepted as you are, you are not loved for your simple being.

If you fulfil their desires they love you; their love is a bargain. If you follow them like shadows, they appreciate, they approve. If you just become a little free and you try to be an individual, they are against you – their eyes, their behaviour, everything changes. And every child is so helpless – just to survive he has to be political, he has to accept whatsoever the parents are saying ... Society is very political. Outside, it posted the policeman and the magistrate; inside it posted the conscience. That is the inner policeman, the inner magistrate.

(Osho, *The Discipline of Transcendence*, Rajneesh Foundation, Pune, India, 1978, vol. 1, ch. 6)

A thorn by any other name...

What Freud calls superego, Osho calls conscience. Other names for this same psychic structure are the inner critic and – a name provided by Zen masters – 'the barking dog'.

The superego is the internalization of all the authority figures of the first years of our life; mostly our parents and their values, judgments, prejudices, admonishments and commandments.

The judge guides our life, creating an undercurrent of judgments, evaluations and admonishments that are constantly present and by which we have to measure ourselves, and our actions, in every aspect of daily life. This undercurrent manifests at all levels of our experience through thoughts, emotions and physical sensations.

At a subconscious level we are constantly engaged in an inner dialogue between a part of ourselves that gives advice, that admonishes, pushes or manipulates us until we behave in a certain way, and another part that reacts to this continual and intense pressure.

The dynamic of this inner dialogue is very similar to that between parents and child: the inner judge treats us as if we were still children – completely dependent, incapable of surviving, and needing constant guidance. The child reacts – by fighting against it, collapsing in scared obedience or freezing in shock and becoming absent and isolated.

Why do we need a superego?

At this point, you may think that there is no point in having a superego, as it only causes pain. But it's important to clearly state the positive side of having a well-structured superego.

This part of the psyche does, in fact, allow us to navigate through daily life with relative ease, providing rules of social behavior that, while obliging us to conform and to distance ourselves from our true nature, allow us to survive.

The downside of these imperatives, reproaches, prejudices and so on is that they radically limit our ability to live fully, love naturally and grow as unique individuals.

With a powerful superego at play, it appears that whatever age we are – 20, 30, 40 years and on – we 'dress with the same clothes' we had when we were 7 or 8 years old. We adopt the same wrappings for our behavior and personalities... and, though inevitably they feel tight, we deny their bad fit. We carry with us a great sense of dissatisfaction and the feeling of not being our 'authentic self'.

Identification

In the inner dynamic of dialogue, conflict and reaction, we side at times with the superego and at other times with the child that reacts. When we are 'siding', this is called identification.

Identification or siding happens automatically and the ego alternately becomes both the parent that orders and manipulates, and the child that reacts. Once this process of identification has been established, it manifests internally as a division of the self into two parts: the part that attacks, and the other that defends itself. Life becomes the exchange between the two.

By internalizing and identifying with their parents, children fulfill two essential functions:

- they create a guiding and control structure (superego) that allows them to keep the unacceptable behaviors in the unconscious
- they guarantee a constant inner presence of the parents and the emotional dynamics that have characterized the relationship with them. From the moment the superego is formed, the ego will have company. It will never be alone again.

Almaas states,

> In time, the external coercive agencies (parents) become internalized. This is done through the processes of introjection and identification, in which the coercive agencies become part of the internal structure of the child. In other words, the child psychically takes in parental demands, and they become his or her own. We must remember that these processes are defensive mechanisms, and they are employed, in this instance, to avoid the loss or expected loss of the parent or his love. So, becoming like the parent acts as a way of having him, and hence as a defense, against losing him; and at the same

time, these defenses are also used to get the parents' love and approval.'

(A. H. Almaas, *Work on the Superego*, Diamond Books, Berkeley CA, USA, 1992, p. 3)

Whether we accept and embrace the values of our parents or we rebel against them, our dependency is essentially unchanged from the moment the superego is formed. The emotional and energetic dynamics that characterized our relationship with our parents continue to reveal themselves in our inner dialogue. This is done in the way we value our behaviors and ourselves, in the way we judge the world around us and in the way we relate with others. Our process of growth is blocked and locked inside repetitive and habitual limits that inhibit our spontaneity and creativity.

Inquiry, meditations and visualizations

1. Investigate the holding environment in your family. What was the atmosphere like in your family when you were a child? What memories do you have of that atmosphere and of yourself in it? How did you feel? What was the environment like where you grew up? Were your parents present in your life? Did you have any physical contact with them, or one of them? What kind? Did you feel supported and recognized, or not? What was appreciated, supported, what were the things considered of value and what was condemned, rejected or hidden?

2. Explore the relationship with authority in your life. How do you relate to authority? Try to isolate the mechanisms, the reactions, the defenses, the judgments that you have towards it. Do you give yourself permission to be an authority? Who were the authority figures in your childhood and how did they show their authority? How did you feel in relation to them?

Chapter 3

Survival and Intrinsic Value

From each according to his ability, to each according to his needs.
Karl Marx, *Critique of the Gotha Program*

It is, perhaps, no longer popular to quote Karl Marx, but this sentence, in my opinion, contains a very beautiful vision of a society based on abundance, and the capacity to satisfy the needs of all; on individual creativity and the possibility to express and realize it. Utopia? Perhaps.

Such an optimistic view of society certainly is idealistic, as long as we are the first to deny our own needs and sabotage our abilities. And sabotage is what happens to every individual who remains bound to an infantile relationship with their own superego.

The superego is a feature, as we saw in the previous chapter, that can be useful. It has a purpose; it was born in answer to the need to survive in a particular family and social environment and has, at its core, the immense energy of the survival instinct. It is our energy and desire to survive, mixed with a fear that we cannot make it without an inner coercive agent, that supports the activity of the superego, and our infantile relationship with it.

With an active superego, no matter how pivotal it is to our survival, we are still caught in a bind. Because of a fundamental lack of trust in our ability to respond in a creative and original way to the circumstances that life presents us with, we tend in fact to re-enact behaviors of the past that are rarely adequate for what happens in the present.

We stop asking ourselves, 'Who am I?' and replace it with 'How should I be?' thereby distorting the attention from our identity (who) to our functioning or behavior (how). In so doing, we conceal reality from ourselves.

Surviving or living?

The superego, if it is well formed, performs the function of survival with a kind of efficiency. But at the same time the superego is not able to help us discover what true 'living' is. In fact, it is an obstacle to living a full life. Surviving and living are very different things – where the first is simply the ability to keep our body/mind system functioning, the second is the ability to create our present and our life, and to be conscious of it.

Surviving is the expression of our animal inheritance; living is the culmination of our humanity. I have not yet met a human being who, consciously or not, doesn't question themselves and their place in the universe, their ability to love and to create, and the sense of their own freedom. These questions and the search for answers are an intrinsic part of life, and most of the conflicts in which we find ourselves are caused by a fundamental confusion between survival and life.

When survival informs our behavior, rather than our felt sense and trust in our humanity (even when there is no threat), we let our superego dictate the laws of how we live, of how we relate with people, and of our behaviors. When this happens we can see that we are not really being human but rather we have fallen back into an infantile state, but without the innocence, the beauty, and the vulnerability of childhood.

Our daily life becomes dictated by, and caught in, a trap of prejudices that prevent us from seeing true reality and force us to behave and react mechanically. Re-acting means to act in the same way as in the past. Reaction means a lack of creativity and spontaneity as well as a lack of consciousness and love.

The fully conscious and alive individual is totally present in the moment and perceives each situation as it is, free from all prejudice and all bias. His perception and his actions are not hampered by emotional or mental preconceptions and are not conditioned by past experiences. Therefore, his perception is accurate and his action is to the point: accordingly, he has the capacity to respond efficiently, in tune with the needs of each situation he encounters ... Although this state is not conceived of by the majority of humanity, it is still a potential for each human being. There is proof enough of its reality in the few individuals of the various spiritual traditions who have realized it. That it's difficult to attain does not negate its possibility. All disciplines truly oriented towards freeing man attempt to realize it. The desire for growth and expansion is, among other things, a direct consequence of the experience of the absence of this condition of freedom, indicating that something necessary – and therefore attainable – is missing.

(A. H. Almaas, *Work on the Superego*, Diamond Books, Berkeley CA, USA, 1992, p. 1)

See yourself

A desire for approval is so intrinsically human and, even when distorted, represents our desire to align ourselves with existence, to feel connected and able to respond in meaningful ways to situations that life presents us with and to optimize our abilities.

Observe how much of your energy is continually engaged in an effort to do 'the right thing' (as defined by yourself), being the things that allow you to feel good and to be acknowledged and appreciated.

But the real question is not to do the right thing. The question is, 'What are the criteria that define what is right or wrong? Right according to whom?' If we look, with a little attention and honesty, it's not difficult to recognize and understand that the rules we tend to live by are set by the inner judge and, therefore, by our internalized parents.

Are we therefore trying to find the right choice for the present moment by means of something that has nothing or little to do with this moment?

Yes, this is exactly what most people are doing.

Being free

How do we read the moment? Our challenge is how to make choices that reflect our consciousness, freedom and originality, based on a non-prejudicial reading of the new and unknown moment that is revealing itself now.

The only way to do this is to redirect our vital energy to be present and to read the signs. What makes this difficult is that in this moment we are almost completely engaged in supporting the dynamic with the superego. So, we need to move from the fear for survival to the discovery of our personal potential and its realization.

So, to move away from this trap we need, simply, to grow up. To grow beyond the dynamics that characterize our relationship with our superego. We need to understand how that dynamic holds us locked in a childish and mediocre condition where, once again, irrespective of our age, we have to answer to our parents. We also need to understand how this dynamic is projected externally onto all our relationships.

Learning to recognize ourselves in the moment, free of the superego, means taking responsibility for making choices not dictated by the past and other people's values, but based on our ability to feel who we really are, what we want and how we intend committing ourselves to realizing our potential.

Defending ourselves against ourselves

Above all, however, being free means learning how to consciously defend ourselves against attacks from the superego, and developing the ability to remain present in the experience while it's happening instead of being drawn into the continuous inner dialogue/conflict between child and parent.

When the vital energy supports our growth, we start to live a life that's not continually striving towards 'how we should be', but is illuminated by the daily discovery of our individuality and uniqueness.

Instead of spending enormous amounts of energy and attention trying to keep a precarious peace between the ego and the superego, we begin to discover who we are, moment by moment, beyond the conditioning received, and discover what abilities and talents this existence has given us.

We begin to discover the joy of recognizing and fulfilling these gifts, and the pleasure of sharing them. We begin to feel that we belong to this life and that this life belongs to us, and so it is our responsibility and our freedom that guides us, not the fear of the inner judge.

[The child's] relationship to his parents not only determines his relationship to himself but also to other people, for it is the prototype of relationships with others and makes its impact on his mind when he is most vulnerable and impressionable. In later years, he relates to people in ways determined by how he related to his parents as a child. The person, then, lives under the tyranny of the past, instead of being free to be present in the moment. This does not mean that the entirety of the individual is conditioned: rather, that the more conditioned a person is, the less accurate are his perceptions, the less appropriate are his actions, and the more pathological is his condition. We see that growth is, at least in part, a process of deconditioning, of freeing parts of the individual that have become arrested by the bonds of repetitive and compulsive ways of responding to life. It is the regaining of the capacity to respond in a fresh manner, instead of reacting in outdated modes.

(Ibid, p. 2)

Acknowledging feelings

For growth to occur, we must first acknowledge that what we feel, what we express and what we aspire to has value. We must therefore be able to perceive our experience with acceptance and in an open way, recognizing its intrinsic value; value that exists simply because it is our experience.

There, as they say, is the rub.

Because it's our superego that decides most of the time what is and what isn't of value in us and in our life, and it's the fear for our own survival that makes us accept the tyranny of the inner judge. Therefore a fundamental part of our journey and our growth is an honest and courageous exploration of our values.

Positive and negative reflections

For most of us, personal worth is dependent on social recognition: if one is judged positively, if there is acceptance, if there is success, if one receives attention, then one has value. We may, too, define our own worth negatively: I am worthy just because I do not fit, I rebel, I am a dropout, and therefore I am refused, judged and rejected.

In both cases, which we call 'positive reflection' and 'negative reflection', an individual's worth depends on the effect that he or she generates externally.

But this dynamic with the outside keeps pace with an internal one where each of us constantly tries to measure our own worth – with the superego and with the values and standards of behavior we consider acceptable.

From our childhood days, we learned to measure our worthiness according to the answer that we received from our parents, so, as adults, the measure of our worth derives from the judge.

We have therefore learnt and continue to believe that we don't have an intrinsic value that is an expression of who we are. Rather we have learnt to hide who we are in order to receive recognition and be valued.

Our original nature, its uniqueness, richness and value are negated in favor of an identity defined by conditioning, and by a value that is reflected from others.

'If you want to have value, you must never be yourself' is a line we have bought over and over again.

Your judge has developed many different standards and beliefs about the parts of your life that are valuable, but its overriding principle that has dominated your life is that you are not intrinsically valuable. You must get value in ways other than just being who you are. As long as you believe this, the judge will have a strong influence over you. If you don't accept the judge's position, then your task is not to learn how to value yourself but to understand why you don't see your inherent value. You don't have to make something happen. You simply need to be curious and explore the fact that you value anything but yourself. Each time you turn toward something else as the source of your value in the moment, you must ask why. How did you learn to value something else more than your own being?

(Byron Brown, *Soul without Shame*, Shambhala Publications, Boston, 1999, p. 230)

When we learn to be present and to defend ourselves against the attacks from the superego, then our consciousness begins to relax. Residing in the present instead of in the past or the future allows us to recognize and to value some aspects of our reality that had previously been hidden by the compulsive activity of our mind.

Then we are able to notice the presence of emotions inside us, of behaviors and desires that for so long have been considered 'unacceptable' by the superego and buried in the unconscious.

This recognition opens the door to personal freedom; the

freedom to decide which of these elements have to be rejected, and which ones have existential value for us, and whether it is worth exploring new possibilities and accepting the responsibility for possible errors and consequences.

Challenging the boundaries imposed by the judge and the values predetermined externally, we begin to expand our territory and regain possession of parts of ourselves that we have avoided for a long time.

As we free ourselves of shame and guilt, inside us we begin to develop trust, and a sense of confidence and direction.

The will to grow and to know yourself will bring you to the discovery of your worth as an individual. The acknowledgment of your intrinsic worth will slowly start to shift from survival to living and to the discovery of the unique qualities of your individuality.

Summing up

No matter whether the result is acceptance and reward, or refusal and punishment, we verify every one of our experiences with the superego, this coercive entity. This is an enormous and exhausting waste of energy.

As long as we are involved in this dynamic with the judge, our sense of personal worth is based on explanations, justifications and a dependence on other people's values.

Each time we shift our attention and awareness from the immediacy of our experience to the inner dialogue/conflict with the superego, we abandon the reality of the present moment and involve ourselves in a repetitive mind game.

This shift objectively devalues our direct experience and makes it dependent on the past and on the historical dynamics with our parents and/or other authority figures in our childhood.

Not only does the immediate experience lose its value but it is also energetically emptied out due to the shift in our attention to the past and to mind games. As the saying goes, we get 'stuck in our head'.

In order to find and recognize the value of our experience it is necessary to develop the ability of being present in the moment with what is happening, either inside us, or outside; resisting and overcoming the habit of commenting, of judging and of classifying our experience by the rules of the past.

Inquiry, meditations and visualizations

1. Explore the theme of survival. What was the attitude of your father and mother in relation to survival?

2. What were the main messages you were given by them? How does this theme manifest in your life? Do you feel relaxed, confident, capable of taking care of yourself and those you love, or are you afraid, do you worry? Observe if you feel any resistance to looking into these matters.

3. Observe in detail the way the issues of survival present themselves in your daily life and what emotions, thoughts and physical sensations are related to it. Let yourself go in this exploration; let go of every judgment that comes to the surface. Give yourself the chance to observe and feel what happens without judging yourself, but at the same time be aware of judgments if they come up.

4. Do you notice any physical symptoms as you explore this survival theme? You may notice particular tensions in your body. If it happens, give yourself time to feel these tensions, where they are located, the density, the shape and the temperature and if there are emotions associated with them.

In many spiritual and energetic maps survival is associated with the area of the pelvic floor and, in particular, with the anus and the perineum (between the anus and the sexual organs); but they are also related to the solar plexus, the shoulders and to the spinal cord. Each of us also has personal ways to psychosomatize, therefore leave your consciousness open to what you feel.

Memories that you didn't know you had may suddenly appear, with images from the past.

Chapter 4

The Inner Judge's Functions

From the moment the inner judge is structured and functions 'efficiently', we are endowed (and stuck) with an inner mechanism that is continuously interpreting and evaluating – us, others, and the events of our daily life.

The superego works by reinforcing the values of the parents and, indeed, all authority figures who had, and perhaps still have, a strong influence on our life.

At the same time the superego, which is 'born' in answer to the need to keep our unacceptable behaviors in the unconscious, becomes the tyrant who controls our actions, emotions and thoughts.

Sometimes we see, with extreme clarity, that we are confined in a prison made of actions, thoughts and behaviors. Sometimes we experience it through a latent sense of impatience and anxiety. And this keeps repeating; we experience a sense of once again being in an unpleasant or painful situation. We may also recognize a feeling of powerlessness and constraint that makes us angry, discontented, resentful and depressed.

Maintaining the status quo

These sensations are related to the first and fundamental function of the superego. Like 'border police', the superego controls the unconscious material – those drives, thoughts, and so on that we suppressed during childhood in order to adapt to the family status quo.

The superego maintains that status quo (now internalized) through a clear division between what is acceptable and what is not. The impulses are so suppressed that they don't reach our consciousness anymore when activated by the events of daily life. Yet the repressed material generally evokes a vague, indefinable sense of anxiety.

This feeling of anxiety is related to behaviors that were considered unacceptable and therefore repressed and are deeply bound to painful states in which we were denied our parents' love.

> This anxiety is a response to the anticipation of danger. In the past, libidinal impulses and accompanying actions, and certain feelings and thoughts and their expression, became perceived as dangerous to the person because of the reactions encountered in the environment to them (especially from the parents) such as disgust, rejection, punishment, abandonment, belittlement, humiliation, judgment, criticism, invalidation, being threatened, doubted, ridiculed, made to feel guilty or shameful, etc. Since the person has learned to anticipate such reactions from the environment in childhood and therefore suppressed himself, he now anticipates the same reactions from his own superego. And the superego does react in this way, because it is the internalization of all these originally external reactions. In other words, the ego relates to the superego just like the child related to the coercive agencies in his environment – afraid of its attacks. So the moment that there is a possibility of unconscious material that drew attacks in the past surfacing to consciousness, the ego responds with anxiety, the danger signal anticipating a superego attack. The ego, to check the emergence of such disapproved of material, employs its defense mechanisms, which result in keeping such material out of consciousness.
>
> (A. H. Almaas, *Work on the Superego*, Diamond Books, Berkeley CA, USA, 1992, p. 3)

Triggers and trauma

Let's look, for example, at the belief that states, 'A person must be strong and not afraid.' This is a very common belief and could have been passed on to us during childhood verbally or energetically through a distancing from father or mother. We may have received the message through humiliation or being teased because we behaved like 'a sissy' when we showed some kind of weakness or fear, or in other ways.

As that was happening, we probably chose to repress every kind of vulnerability that could appear to be a weakness and to put on a brave face; so as to avoid the painful state of losing our parents' love and/or to gain their approval.

In the years following the initial repression, the superego's task is to prevent these unacceptable responses (fear and weakness) from surfacing. The superego will attack us each time these responses reach our consciousness.

When, as an adult, the circumstances of daily life confront us and we feel vulnerable, we instantly associate this with the emotions of fear and weakness and, immediately, memories of the specific fears and weaknesses that were repressed in childhood are activated and generate an 'incomprehensible' anxiety.

At that point, the ego intervenes to block the anxiety and any repressed material related to it which might surface from the unconscious. It does this through judgments of oneself and others directing us towards the image of strength and invulnerability with which one has identified. We then reconfirm that this strength has become a fundamental part of our personality.

The most common result of the inner dynamic as the ego tries to avoid the superego's attacks, is that we become incapable of contacting our own, or another's, vulnerability.

This lack, in turn, means we have a limited perception of our inner world – we exclude all and any manifestations deemed not to be 'strong' and we most probably adopt a (false) sense of superiority.

The ego forces us to maintain an image of strength despite the fact that we know logically (and emotionally) that it is impossible to always be strong. The pretence prevents us from perceiving our own or others' finer feelings – those that have to do with sensitivity, openness and flexibility.

But because the superego's action is repressive, it inevitably contains an aggressive energy, which can be direct, working through orders, commands and reproaches, or indirect, through manipulation and guilt feelings.

There are physical responses too – we may face this aggressiveness, for example, by tightening the solar plexus (two inches below the breast bone), pushing the chest out and tautly straightening the spine; becoming 'hard' and, later, projecting our fear and vulnerability onto other people by attacking them for their weakness, further reinforcing our image of 'strength' to the outside world.

The superego – in its role as defender of the status quo – manages our survival by regulating and controlling the energetic level of our body's system, forcing life to go on in a zone where there is neither too much vitality and excitement, nor too many unknown or difficult situations to manage. The superego leads us towards those ideals that, according to it, make us acceptable and successful people.

In this role as regulator, the superego repeats the maternal and paternal role of the first years of life.

Establishing a self-image

A second role of the superego is to give us a sense of identity based on self-image. Our identity is based on a constant and repetitive 'inner dialogue' which has us enumerating our values, opinions and points of view, alongside a web of tensions at a physical level and our particular emotional state.

We wake up in the morning and we recognize ourselves by the inner dynamics with the judge, our troubles, our desires, our emotional make-up, our opinions and our tensions.

[The self-image] is much more than merely the social mask we present to others. It also includes our inner view of ourselves and our body image. The self-image is not innate but develops through our interactions with the world, significant others, and our bodies. We come to be attached to our self-image, and we take it to be who (and all) we really are. We all use a wide variety of mental structures, memories, plans, and images to conduct our lives successfully. To be most useful, our mental representations need to be in touch with reality. When we approach any situation with a fixed structure based on past experiences, we are bound to be somewhat out of touch with the reality of the present situation. Our perceptions, behaviors, and relationships will be less responsive, less appropriate, and less effective. By the same token, they will also be more reactive, more forced, and more frustrating. The basic nature of the mind is space, unstructured and open. This means, too, that our underlying experience of ourselves will be spacious and open to whatever arises in this space. When we identify with mental structures and their underlying boundaries, however, this space becomes bounded and restricted. The self-image is the collection and integration of those structures and boundaries that are developed in the process of ego development. The self-image, then, is the sum total of those mental structures that we use to define ourselves.

(John Davis, *The Diamond Approach*, Shambhala Publications, Boston, 1999, pp. 63, 64)

V.'s story

V. is a young painter, aged 40. She is attractive, vivacious and intelligent. For the past few years since her marriage break-up, V. has been sincerely committed to her personal development. She married when she was very young and had her first son at 19.

She was raised in a traditionalist, observant Roman Catholic family who viewed any sexual activity before marriage as a sin, as something to be condemned. An essential part of her inner and outer image is the one of 'the good girl', reliable, empathetic, helpful.

V. is exploring the difficulties of her relationships with men; the reasons she feels betrayed and deserted; her difficulty in communicating her needs and her tendency to dramatize situations. She is looking at how these relate to various aspects of her relationship with her parents. In a session with me, V. tells some of her story:

'At the age of 16, I mixed with people older than me and I felt important – I was a young girl in my third year of high school while my friends attended university. One of them liked me and I became his "girlfriend". I believed I was in love with him too; but he cheated on me continuously with other women and then he told me he was in love with my cousin, and that was the reason he had chosen me!

I went on summer holiday and out of spite I behaved like him and got pregnant. This is where the lies began: I did all I could to make him believe that the baby was his. At first he didn't believe me, but I was so clever at planting the seeds of doubt that he proposed to me!

I won't deny the idea was very enticing, but I didn't want that baby. I only wanted my parents not to find out, and I wanted him to pay for the abortion, which was then illegal. We didn't have the money so we devised a plan to tell my parents that I had been raped. This meant also that I wasn't guilty.

Then began a life of hell.

Imagine my parents' pain at the thought of their daughter being raped, and their pain at the idea of me having an abortion, something they considered to be murder.

My father wasn't entirely convinced of my story and subjected me to a nerve-wracking "third degree". He wanted to know the details and the circumstances; I should have won the Oscar for Best Actress because I convinced him, but he made me sign a paper in which I assumed responsibility for the abortion, so that I would never be able to accuse him of being my baby's murderer. They found a doctor who was willing to operate on me in return for a generous fee.

The whole thing took a few hours and at the end of it, my mother took me home. The following morning I went to school and we never ever spoke about it. It was as if it never happened.'

The internalization

This is just one of the episodes that happened to V. that have resulted in her accommodating people (mostly men), putting aside and hiding her truth. Because of this episode, too, she allows men 'to do as they please' as long as they love her.

Her inner judge strongly intervenes to keep in place the image of a 'respectable' girl, and to put aside, 'for her own good and that of others', anything that could cause her to be rejected. This rigid image, and her relation with the superego compel her to hide parts of her personality considered unacceptable and this unconscious need to be 'excused' for what she is (very different from what she appears). It compels her to 'excuse' others.

She continues her story:

'Through continuous inquiry into myself, I have discovered that my tendency to find "justifications and absolution" for everyone, even towards those who don't treat me as I'd like and who hurt me (not only once but many times), doesn't derive from a true feeling of compassion, understanding and forgiveness, as I have always believed, but from the absolute and primary need to "absolve and pardon" me for past events that have determined not only the course of my life but also that of my son...'

Setting limits

The third function assumed by the superego is related to boundaries and limits.

The superego, through its judgments, creates a condition of constant duality, where everything is divided into good and bad, into what is acceptable and what is to be condemned, what is moral and what isn't...

In each duality, the superego will identify the outer limit, a boundary beyond which it is not permissible to go. Inevitably, this boundary becomes a battle zone, sometimes conscious, but in most cases on an unconscious level.

Each time we go near the boundary line, we feel anxious, and this anxiety triggers the superego to intervene. The superego will do all it can to bring us back to the known territory, to behavior that is considered acceptable.

These boundaries are very real energetic structures which express themselves in our body and influence our senses.

The net of boundaries and limits works effectively and we begin to read all our reality through conditioned perceptions – as if wearing a pair of glasses with lenses of a certain color. In particular, these boundaries give us a specific perception of the space inside us and around us.

A safety net or a constraint?

You might have noticed that in moments of relaxation, when the process of judging is absent or minimal, your perception of space expands and you have, at the same time, a sensation of being able to breathe easier. You feel as if you have 'more space'.

This is not merely a mental impression or a fantasy, but rather a real experience that has to do with the temporary dissolving of the rigid limits imposed by the superego and of the self-image that is formed by the structuring of those borders in space and in the body.

Knowing who we are

We recognize ourselves because we are one way and not another. We recognize ourselves, therefore, through a dividing line. For example we say, 'I'm strong and not weak', 'I'm extroverted and not introverted', 'I'm capable of finishing my projects and I don't leave things half done', and so on.

Each time life presents us with a situation that challenges our identity and boundaries (for example, situations in which we feel weak or where we don't want to communicate but rather want to close ourselves off and lick our wounds), we will unconsciously reject that situation. Of course, we can't accept this 'label' of weak, nor can we show it, so each time we are in this kind of situation a battle starts inside us – the superego works in order for our image of a strong, extroverted and capable person to remain in place.

Integration is possible

If we are able (through inquiry and our ability to be in the here/now), to resist the superego's pressure to reinforce our image, and we allow ourselves the chance to explore and feel other possibilities – to be weak or introverted or incompetent – the boundaries will tend to fade, becoming less defined and rigid. When our self-image becomes more flexible, less solid and dense, we develop a more fluid personality structure that is more able to respond to situations rather than reacting in predetermined ways.

We begin then to integrate parts of ourselves that we have for a long time denied or rejected, and start to let them grow.

Whether our paths take us into psychotherapy, spiritual work, or self-guided experiments with consciousness exploration, two states soon arise. First, we generally find a sense of emptiness, deficiency, disorientation, or weakness. We discover that much of our everyday experience is discolored by a feeling of constriction or a subtle kind of imprisonment. Our lives seem founded in limitations: everywhere we turn are boundaries. We also eventually find a sense of spaciousness. It may be the result of an emotional release or the consequence of a deep insight. It might occur suddenly with a discharge of tension, or it might slowly creep into the periphery of our awareness. This spacious state brings an openness, an expansion, and a relief from constrictions. It is accompanied by a lightness, a greater sense of internal freedom, a reduction of mental anguish, and a sense of much greater potential and possibility than we have known before. We may come to discover pretty early in our search that giving space to our experience helps. Whether it is physical pain, emotional distress, anger in a relationship, or confusion, when we let there be space in our experience, it moves. We discover as well that when we try to reject or avoid our suffering, it only gets more entrenched. We see that space is on our side.

(Ibid, p. 62)

Revelation can be scary

It's not an easy moment when we realize we don't have the slightest idea who we really are once we take off the mask.

It is important to say that this experience of manifesting 'space' in our consciousness and the dissolving or loosening of inner barriers and boundaries is often a very deep process. The process forces us to confront all the concepts and ideas we have about ourselves, revealing to us their groundlessness, abstractness and the degree to which they depend on values assumed from the outside.

And, at the same time, in my experience with hundreds of spiritual seekers, in that moment of deep realization I have always witnessed the appearance of a sense of relief together with excitement and curiosity.

The question, 'Who am I?' takes on life and is motivated by a genuine desire to know ourselves beyond the conditioning we have received.

Rewarding and punishing

The last of the superego's functions has to do with rewarding and punishing.

From a very young age we experienced some behaviors as acceptable, and they were supported and rewarded. Others, on the other hand, were refused, condemned and punished.

As we have seen in previous chapters, the internalization of our parents and other authority figures leads to the formation of the superego, the inner authority. And through the various forms of 'You must' or 'You must not' the superego rules all aspects of our behavior and of our inner life.

We have in our psyche an effective mechanism that rewards or punishes us according to how we relate to its commands. If we obey, we are rewarded; if we rebel, we are punished.

What is the reward? It is a sense of easiness and the temporary disappearance of anxiety (that has usually been activated by the arising of 'forbidden' behaviors and desires) as we drive them back into the unconscious, together with the manifesting of the superego's approval for that act of self-repression. It is a pat on the shoulder, a puffing up of our ego...

The punishment? It will be feelings of guilt, shame, rejection, neglect, disgust, humiliation... for re-experiencing sensations and emotions associated with those prohibited behaviors and desires felt as a child.

We can then say that the presence of guilt, shame and rejection of ourselves are symptoms of the presence of an inner conflict between ego and superego. We can also say that anxiety – the alarm bell activated by the unconscious 'stuff' that pushes toward the surface – is our main door for reconnecting with that material suppressed in childhood.

Ring the alarm bell

One way to proceed, in order to find out and to understand the way the superego works inside us, is to use the anxiety as the entrance door.

If we accept that everyone lives with a certain level of anxiety and that a certain amount is not in and of itself destructive, we need to discern when to use that anxiety as a trigger for change. In some situations our anxiety levels rise quickly and it would be this moment when it would be important to search and explore all possible causes and associations with this anxiety.

The hardest step is the first one: to be consciously aware of the anxiety that surfaces, and to be able to be present with it without denying, avoiding, repressing or escaping it in any way. A basic support is given by continuing to focus on our body and follow the thread of the experience while it's occurring, and notice how our body's perception of tensions changes.

Consciousness is full of light and love and it won't be difficult for you to feel that, simply by staying present in the experience, even as the more negative and oppressive emotions can be slowly released, often revealing unexpected significance and insight.

When doing inquiry we can feel what kind of associations are in the body and what kind of tensions reveal themselves; we can feel the physical and energetic presence of defense mechanisms and their emotional content; we can become aware of specific attacks from the judge and of their content, specifically self-judgment or judgment of others. We can note the appearance of images and memories from childhood and of family situations or situations at school where those judgments were shaped and consolidated, and so on.

Inquiry, meditations and visualizations

1. Have you noticed emotional situations in your life that tend to repeat themselves? For example, do you have behaviors you know are not useful? Do you react in certain

situations in known and predictable ways? Do you re-create external situations that seem to repeat similar situations from the past? Are some of your emotions reactive and compulsive?

If you answered 'Yes' to any of these questions, describe them in detail with their physical, emotional and mental components. Include also the images and judgments associated with these components.

What do you feel when you talk about them? Do you justify yourself, is there frustration, resignation, is there the will to escape or to fight, or something else?

2. Consider your inner program of what is acceptable and what is not and complete the following lists. In the first list, write 'How I should be'. Take a full 10 minutes, remembering that everything that comes to the surface is important, even items that seem of little significance. In the second list, write 'How I should not be'. Take a full 10 minutes for this list too.

3. Explore how you block your life force, your vitality. Note the situations in which this happens, the circumstances, the types of people you may be with, and where you feel it in your body. How do you feel when this happens? Do you get angry with yourself? Do you justify yourself? Do you put off a situation until the future? Do you pretend nothing happened? What else?

4. Explore your anxiety. What do you know of it? What kind of attitude do you have towards your anxiety? Do you condemn yourself because of it? Do you try to make it go away? In which ways do you avoid it? Be precise: alcohol, sex, food, shopping, work, friends, worrying, meditation, shifting your attention to the outside, television. How does it manifest in your body?

Part 2

Freedom from the Judge

Chapter 5

Defending against Attacks from the Inner Judge

From the time we are young we develop ways to defend ourselves from the superego and to avoid – as much as possible – the pressure it causes.

These defenses of the ego are unconscious and automatic and involve a certain level of habitual tension. We need to be on the alert, to be constantly ready to respond to attacks and criticisms, in order for these defenses to function. This means a constant level of paranoia, a continual readiness to counterattack or to run away.

Our fundamental response to any danger – perceived or real – is fight or flight. This mechanism is always activated in response to advanced states of alert. The more powerful the material that surfaces from the unconscious (and the stronger the demarcation between what is acceptable and what's not), the higher the level of alert and the higher the level of fear of imminent attack from the superego will be.

Habitual unconscious defenses

The first part of our work with the superego is to become aware of our habitual defense mechanisms; the ways we manage to block attacks from the judge before they happen, as well as the ways we react once these attacks have happened.

At the beginning, the external world, particularly the parents, is the primary coercive agency that influences the ego and conditions it to be one way or another ... For the ego to listen and obey the demands of the external agencies (to avoid their displeasure and to gain their love and approval), the ego develops ways to check and control certain of the impulses of the organism. These methods are what are called the ego's defense mechanisms. They are defenses against the impulses of the id (the largely unconscious seat of the instincts in the psyche), and whatever thoughts, fantasies, and sensations that cluster around them or point to them. But they are, as we see, ultimately defenses against the coercive agencies, instituted to defend against their punishments and to please them.

(A. H. Almaas, *Work on the Superego*, Diamond Books, Berkeley CA, USA, 1992, pp. 2, 3)

Our defenses are directly linked to the attacks we receive in childhood; linked to the contents of the attacks, as well as to our fear or expectation of those attacks. So, an effective way to become aware of the defenses is to explore how our superego attacks us and how we act in relation to those attacks.

Three modes of unconscious defense

Broadly speaking, defenses fall into three categories: attack, escape, or freeze. In most cases all these modes are present in us, though most of us have one favorite that generally arrives first. Are you mostly a fighter, a flighter, or someone who gets frozen?

Having defenses is not problematic in itself. They are useful – who wants a pest breathing down their neck day and night? But it is their nature that causes problems. Our defenses are, in the main, unconscious and automatic. They are also motivated and sustained by fear.

When we were children we found intelligent ways to defend ourselves against attacks and not feel the hurt – first from parents, and then from the superego. Perhaps we stopped communicating our feelings and we found a place to hide and disappear, or we threw tantrums to get the denied attention. Perhaps we became very quiet and looked absorbed or rebellious or manipulating. Or we became the smiling 'good boy' or 'good girl'.

These defenses allowed us space to maneuver internally and externally without having to reckon with control from the superego all the time. They also allowed us not to feel too anxious or to be too pained by the fact that we denied parts of ourselves. To avoid suffering from the forgetting, we relegated our responses to the cellar of our unconscious.

At the same time, these defenses – anger, withdrawal or an autistic mode – reflected, in their substance and in the way they operated, the knowledge, the strength and the understanding of a child at a pre-adolescent level of maturity. They also reflected a situation in which children were completely dependent on their parents for survival and had to adapt to being regulated by them or risk punishment, rejection and isolation or even physical and emotional harm.

Maturing and becoming independent

Today, however, those of you reading these pages are no longer children. In all probability, you are no longer dependent on your parents for survival, and your body is not in mortal danger if someone else doesn't take care of it.

If you are here, reading this, and if you care about yourself, your superego has performed its function efficiently, guaranteeing your survival and, at the same time, giving you some mental and emotional tools that demand you to live, not merely survive.

You are engaging with these ideas because:

- you ask questions
- you are aware of a division that causes conflict and uncertainty inside you
- your consciousness demands to know yourself better
- you are curious and, most likely, want more from life
- love burns inside you.

Perhaps it also means that you are ready to take responsibility for growing up and letting go of the superego's hand.

There are precise steps that help us on this path to letting go; help us break the compulsive nature of the dynamic between ego and superego. We can learn to consciously defend ourselves, to free and to integrate increasingly more parts of our unconscious and, ultimately, move beyond the inner division between control and freedom.

Identifying and disidentifying

There are two processes through which we create the superego – internalization and identification. As we saw in Chapter 2, for the superego to function it's necessary that we completely identify with it; we have to believe, with absolute conviction, that we are the judge.

But in reality, in daily life, we continue to alternate our identification – between the judge and the child that is reacting to the attack. This is where the reactions of fight, flight or freeze are activated.

A clear demonstration of the identification process is the language we use when we express this dichotomy. We say, 'A part of myself says that I should... and another part...' This is precisely what happens internally.

We hear voices, we feel emotions, we see images and have contradictory feelings that divide us in two or more parts, and we identify with 'a part of us' (the superego and its dictates) or 'another part of us' (the child that reacts). This dynamic happens through an inner movement, which we call 'attachment'.

When the father says: 'Don't do this, I don't accept this, I am angry about this' – when he punishes a child because he thinks he has done something wrong, what is he doing? When he appreciates the child, gives him a toy, brings flowers for him, sweets, and says: 'You have done well, you have done something good of which I approve' – what is he doing? He is creating a division in the child. By and by the child will also reject the part that the parents have rejected, and he will be divided: he will become two I's. You may have observed little children – they even punish themselves; they even say to themselves: 'Bobby, this is not good. You have done a bad thing.' They start rejecting the part that has been rejected by their parents. Then a division is created. The rejected part becomes the unconscious, the suppressed part; and the accepted part becomes the conscious, the conscience. Then their whole life will be a hell, because the rejected and the accepted will go on fighting; continuously there will be a turmoil.

(Osho, *My Way: The Way of the White Clouds*, Rajneesh Foundation, Pune, India, 1977, ch. 14)

Defending oneself – consciously

The first step to defending ourselves against the superego is, perhaps, the most difficult. It is to become aware of the judge and the judging and to recognize when we are under attack. It is difficult because of the identification that automatically leads us to accept that the judgments, the evaluations, the pressures we feel inside and the effects they produce (guilt, shame, indecision, lack of self-value) are the expression of a 'part' of ourselves, rather than an automatic and unconscious effect of the superego's activity.

The superego is, fundamentally, a mechanism, a program that is constantly re-proposing that which has already been conveyed by the original coercive agencies (mother and father mainly) and other authority figures (older siblings, grandparents, teachers, priests etc.) with whom the child interacted while growing up.

The simplest way to know we are under attack is to recognize the symptoms of that attack – feelings of guilt, shame, stress, scorn, insecurity, depletion of energy, tension in the body, a sudden rage; feelings of invisibility and paralysis, shock, confusion and, of course, anxiety. These are only some of the possible symptoms and your search will be to find, with the greatest possible care, which of them are yours. Sometimes when we recognize the symptoms we realize that we have been under attack for days, or months, and sometimes even years.

The closer we get to recognizing and identifying the major symptoms, the sooner we'll be able to recognize attacks from the superego. The goal is to recognize the attack exactly in the moment it happens and be able to consciously defend against it.

Anthony's story

Anthony works as a software programmer for a mobile phone company. He is a young Scotsman of great sensitivity and technical expertise.

This is how his superego attacked him, recently, in the workplace:

'I got up to take the work I had organized to my supervisor. I had worked like fury to develop this software with my team and we had done a fantastic job. To say we were pleased is an understatement. I was feeling really proud of my and our creativity, and of our commitment.

While I was going up in the lift to the floor where technical management is located, I suddenly felt something like a stone in my solar plexus and a wave of thoughts and anxieties. Doubts about the job I had done and about the product we developed filled my head and I felt my stomach and buttocks contract and my knees give way.

Fortunately I was alone and had a few minutes to understand what was happening to me.

Having done some "inquiry" work in the previous months, in regard to the superego and my insecurities at work, instead of pretending as if nothing happened as I usually do, I paid attention to what was happening to me and I recognized the symptoms of a superego attack and the judgment that upheld it: "It will go badly for you, you'll see. You know that you're not able to present things. Do you remember the last time? You nearly lost your job. Maybe it's better if you say you need more time."

This story is a real drag! I know it by heart and it eats away at me and I usually end up running away and postponing, and looking indecisive and not up to the job. I took a deep breath and focused my attention on my feet and the feeling of the floor supporting me – even if it was moving! Instead of going back and forth in my head and engaging in an all too familiar tit-for-tat, I decided to remain present in my body and continue to feel the sensations that would emerge and how they changed.

Thanks to the inquiry work, I recognized my inner atmosphere as similar to when I was a child and what I felt when my father came back from work: he looked so hangdog. That memory fills me with sadness and rage at the same time.

My solar plexus seems to relax and the breathing slows down a little. Also the shoulders relax. It is also as if my weight is falling with more force on my feet and I definitely have a clearer perception of my legs. The voice inside has not disappeared but seemed further away, at the periphery of my attention.

Suddenly, something explodes inside me like a thought, an emotion and a feeling all at the same time, like a voice that shouts: "I have done a good job! Or, rather, an excellent job!" I feel my face flush.

Oh God! The lift stops and the door opens; for a second I feel like a tree in the wind and panic-stricken! But the feeling inside me is strong. I have done a good job. I know it. I honestly have no doubts. Even my colleagues know it and I am here for me and for them.

I stop at the drinking fountain for a drop of water, and that sip is as if it dissolves everything inside. I feel whole and confident; mostly I feel it on my forehead. In those following steps I feel there is also something else and this surprises me: I am excited at the idea of presenting my work!'

Recognize, reflect, disidentify

There are a lot of useful elements in Anthony's description. I would like you, however, to note the passage where Anthony, recognizing the symptoms in his body, decides to pay attention to those symptoms. In so doing he becomes aware of a voice that is judging him and he knows those judgments too well because they have recurred several times in the past, and in similar circumstances.

Thanks to the work he has already done, Anthony is able to recognize in a following session with me that those judgments come from his mother and were the judgments she had with regard to her husband. He also knows that his mother threw him into doubt every time he wanted to do something that she didn't want and that, in those situations, he felt very similar physical feelings to the ones he experienced in the lift.

Drawing his attention to his body and to the associated emotions, Anthony is able to feel these judgments about himself and recognize where they come from. This allows him to create a space, a separation between himself – the subject of the experience – and the judgments and energy of the attack: this space is the beginning of disidentification.

In recognizing the original source of those judgments (his mother), the space becomes bigger and so too the distance between Anthony (subject) and the attack (object). This distance enables him to decide not to react to the attack with his usual patterns (by collapsing and losing confidence and clarity), but to remain present in the moment.

This technique is very powerful.

By returning your energy and thought to whatever is happening to you in the present, you can completely interrupt the habitual nature of the process of identification with the superego. And be on your way to a freedom from that judgment and control.

Inquiry, meditations and visualizations

1. Sit for a while with your eyes closed, feeling your body – how you sit, breathe, what feelings you have in your legs and arms. How do you feel inside in this moment? Don't force yourself to relax or to do anything special; simply be yourself, as you are.

   After a few minutes, open your eyes. Ask, 'What are the most serious judgments I have about myself?' For 10 minutes, voice the judgments you have towards:

   - your body
   - your sexuality
   - your intelligence
   - your relationship with power
   - your relationship with money
   - your relationship with work
   - the way you relate with others
   - your spirituality
   - any other aspect that comes to mind.

Express yourself without the pressure that what you say must make sense, and without censoring or choosing one thing rather than another. The judgment, 'I am too thin' is just as important as the one that says, 'I can't express myself' or 'I am not able to have a lasting relationship' or 'I get blinded by jealousy'. Let the judgments surface.

If possible, do this inquiry with a partner. If you don't have a partner, do the inquiry in front of a mirror.

2. After 10–15 minutes, include in your field of attention the things you notice in your body.

In particular, note if there are places of tension. Note where they are, what kind of tension it is, how deep it is, if it has a shape, a color, a temperature. Notice if there are parts of your body you can't feel. Once you have rapport with your body, begin to observe the emotions that are present.

3. How do you feel in regard to those judgments? What is your first reaction? Are you angry, deflated? Do you want to run away? Are you sad?

   What do you do to silence the judge? What would you like to do in order to silence the judge? Do memories surface – perhaps of your mother or your father who said similar things? How did you feel on those occasions? Continue communicating your immediate experience and try to identify the defense mechanism.

4. After a further 10 minutes, close your eyes and turn your complete attention to your body, letting go of everything else if possible.

You will most probably feel sensations and tensions that are familiar to you and which you have already experienced in the past as blockages or contractions in different parts of your body: tension in the shoulders, or the solar plexus, a contraction of the genitals or a lump in your throat and so on. Simply observe whatever you find; feel it without doing anything to change it. These are 'symptoms' associated to the attacks of the superego, to specific judgments, and to our defenses. Make a brief note of the symptoms and other relevant things.

Chapter 6

The Pillars of Conscious Defense

If we want to learn how to defend ourselves from the judge's attacks, and to begin to explore our potential as individuals, we need to understand the mechanism of identification and to start an inverse process: disidentification.

Inevitably, when we start to move in this direction we need to be very aware of our attachment to our own inner images, our opinions, and the emotions associated with them. We can also notice our attachment to a certain vision of the reality surrounding us, our prejudices, moral values, and the absoluteness and the presumption of correctness of our convictions.

Our inner world and all our relationships with the outside world are based on and defined by our inner relationship with the judge. A large component of the judge is formed by the values we have received from our family, religious and social conditioning.

A fundamental dilemma presents itself to us, a dilemma that has a real foundation and can generate timidity. The questions we are faced with are: 'If I start to be myself, to break certain rules and behavior, if I let my spontaneity show by saying what I think and what I feel, will I be accepted and acknowledged or will I be rejected and denied?' And, in the last instance, 'Will that mean I remain alone?'

These questions and the fears they contain have a real basis: the fact that since childhood, our authentic being has been rejected and condemned. We were taught that we can't be ourselves, that we must hide 'unacceptable' behaviors or be punished.

Added to that, from the beginning of humanity, the most powerful punishments have been banishment and isolation, which cause strong feelings of loneliness. At the same time we feel inside us an irresistible need to expand, to know ourselves and to fulfill our nature: to know our soul and have a sense of self.

Who am I?

We all need to ask the primary questions, 'Who am I?' and 'What is life?' These are questions that agitate inside every one of us, whether we are aware of them or not. Even if we determinedly pursue external objects and desires, many people in reflective moments long for an answer to these questions and the true peace that that may bring.

These questions are the motor of evolution for the individual and humanity, and run continually in our veins. Everything we do, every breath, every love, the desire for success, orgasm, creative passion, the thirst for power, our intensity in pursuing an ideal, our religiosity, all our aspirations have only one purpose, whether we are aware of it or not: to know who we are and what we are doing here.

The superego gives us ground on which we base our survival and social functioning. At the same time it is the most immediate obstacle to a direct experience of our nature and its depth beyond the structure of personality.

It is on the razor's edge of this understanding that we walk during the process of disidentification from the judge and towards the discovery and understanding of our attachment.

Recognizing limits is the start of growth

When we recognize the limits imposed by the judge, our fear of solitude, the need to be accepted, and our desire for freedom and authenticity, then we begin to grow.

We need to move away from the compulsive domination of

the inherited and acquired values of conditioning, to find our own values, based on our experience and intelligence. We need to find the ability to consciously use the acquired values when we consider them relevant.

We don't have to destroy the judge, but rather to expand the field of our experience and be able to push back the borders that define us, to expand our awareness and challenge the rigidity of conditioned values.

Now, much of what the judge 'says' is very useful. A judge who tells us not to undress in a public place, or to be careful of the pedestrians walking on the pedestrian crossing is, definitely, useful.

When that same judge attacks us telling us that we should perform better in anything we are doing – making love, for example – or taunts us that our sex organs are inadequate, or that it's better not to open up in order to avoid being hurt because 'men only want one thing anyway', then we are subject to judgments, prejudices and a load of criticism and aggression that is certainly not useful to us.

The only effect of these kinds of judgments is to separate us from what we are experiencing, what we are living. They take us to an abstract world of values and opinions based on the past, and disallow any change based on intelligent understanding and our growing capacity to respond to what is happening here and now.

Growth derives from finding an adult relationship with this entity that, in the commendable attempt to give us direction and help us survive, continues to treat us as if we were children.

Many therapeutic and growth disciplines can be seen as different ways of getting through the ego resistances to unconscious material, although some approaches reject this terminology. The classical approaches see ego resistances as defenses against the id impulses: while in our work, especially in the initial stages, we see them as defenses against the superego. The superego, as we have seen, is the first coercive agency that we encounter in working on ourselves, which we find to be invested in keeping the unconscious, unconscious and which accomplishes this by disapproving of the unconscious material. So, our approach is to help the ego consciously defend itself against the attacks of the superego, and hence to eliminate this important part of the need for unconscious defense mechanisms. If this is done, some awareness of feelings and sensations will bring up the part of the unconscious disapproved of by the superego, now that the ego is not guarding against it. This in turn will bring up other attitudes of the superego, which the person can learn to work with. Deeper layers of the unconscious will surface, like those related to painful ego states or to the elements of the ego structure. This process can continue until all repressed material becomes conscious, which means that all hidden prejudices are recognized and dealt with; and in this way the superego loses all of its coercive power. In this stage of working on oneself, the ego turns against the superego, instead of against the id or the other repressed parts of the soul.

(A. H. Almaas, *Work on the Superego*, Diamond Books, Berkeley CA, USA, 1992, p. 6)

Will: The solid mountain

In order for us to turn against the superego, the ego needs to have two qualities above all others: will and strength.

Will gives us a strong determination and commitment to want to know ourselves, together with the ability to support ourselves during the long journey of self-discovery.

It also gives us the confidence that is necessary to look the monster in the eyes, continuing to remain present in the moment, instead of engaging our attention in compulsive dynamics with the superego. The will supports our desire for freedom and enables us to reject the superego's flattery and avoid its traps.

Faisal Muqaddam is the creator, with A. H. Almaas, of the 'Diamond Approach to Self-Realization' – a vast and very articulate view of the relation between personality, soul and True Nature of Reality. This includes and correlates ancient spiritual wisdom and modern in-depth psychology.

In his teaching Muqaddam uses a mythic example of the way the will supports us to face the superego, through the story of Moses and his will, his choice to take his people out of Egypt to the Promised Land, refusing the offers of power, riches and divinity from the pharaoh. *(Faisal Muqaddam led his first European training on The Lataif – the map of the qualities of Essential Nature in the Sufi tradition – in Tuscany in 1997. On that occasion he associated a particular prophet with each quality of Essence according to Arabic mysticism. The prophet of the White Essence or Will Essence is Moses.)*

'Will' gives us a distinct sensation that we have put ourselves and our growth in first place instead of in constant conflict with the inner authority.

'Will' is love of the truth that takes the place of habit and repetition in our relationship with the judge. It is a sense of detachment and tranquillity that doesn't deny the presence of the judge, and doesn't react like a defenseless child.

But 'will' is also the ability to recognize if and when we have been carried away. When we are in contact with our will, we don't allow ourselves to be lured by the attacks or manipulations of the judge, we don't succumb to shame or guilt, we don't hurry to find ways to hide ourselves from what is going on.

On the contrary, we give ourselves time and space to feel and to recognize what is happening; we consciously detach from judgments and support our desire to know ourselves. We do this by breathing more slowly, feeling our body, and listening, in a relaxed way, to the judge's voice.

When we are in contact with our will, we put our life, our

experience, our being at the center. We recognize that our freedom can't be bought and a great sense of dignity and integrity fills us, making us solid and grounded, aware of the moment-to-moment unfolding experience.

In many martial arts traditions, the ability to remain present and relaxed in the face of an attack is an essential condition for the development of any defense or counterattack. It is also considered the beginning and the end of the journey: imperturbable presence, 'detachment'.

The great masters of Aikido, Tai Chi, Qigong, Sword and many other martial arts, continuously invite disciples to observe themselves while the attack is coming, and not to give way to anxiety and the desire to anticipate the next moment. The emphasis is on a relaxed intensity, similar to that of the cat in front of the mouse hole – waiting relaxed but alert, confident in its abilities, with its senses on full alert.

If we practice 'detachment', we do not identify with the attack or let it catch all our attention to the exclusion of all else. Nor do we allow the usual reaction determined by the past and by fear. Detachment requires that we are neither the superego nor the child who reacts.

The most effective ways to get in touch with our will are the techniques of centering and grounding that help us focus our attention on the body – and in particular the belly. The belly is considered the energy center of will. Techniques that focus our awareness on the belly connect us to our will. In Appendix B at the end of the book you will find many simple techniques that can help you in centering and grounding.

Strength: The lion-heart

Being present is a powerful experience but is not, unfortunately, sufficient in most cases to stop the superego's attacks and to eradicate this coercive mechanism.

The judge is, fundamentally, aggressive and oppressive and

for years this fear of being attacked has forced us to direct our rage against our impulses. These impulses (called the id in Freudian terminology) have been driven back into the unconscious, resulting in repression of our vitality.

When we make developing our defense from the superego the center of the work on ourselves, the ego can learn to 'redirect' its rage and aggressiveness against the superego. This is a fundamental step to freeing our vital force and to regaining possession of the passion for living. It also aligns us with a life beyond mere survival and the management of a mediocre daily life.

This 'redirecting' is also a fundamental step in confronting our unconscious fear of the judge and the tension that it produces inside us, and to begin to recognize our courage. It is not sufficient to 'pull the plug' on automatic reactivity; it is also important to express our individuality and our right to take on responsibility for our life, to choose our path, to live our choices, to make our own mistakes, to learn our lessons, to fall down and to get up again.

When we develop the ability to direct our aggressiveness against the judge in defense of our life, then we discover our true strength. By freeing our aggressiveness we relight the flame of our passion and vitality. It is in our ability to separate ourselves from the superego's tyranny that an inner force is liberated, and in turn becomes the vehicle for freeing increasingly vast parts of our unconscious.

Faisal Muqaddam, when talking about the prophet associated with this part of the search and manifestation of the true force, mentions David – the Jewish prince – and his fight with Goliath. Goliath is the symbol of the superego and represents the barrier between us and freedom.

Another relevant mythic image is that of Medusa, the monster of Greek mythology, with the body of a woman and snakes instead of hair. The snakes represent the judgments and prejudices of the superego, and, as in the myth, every time we cut the head of a snake it grows again. Every time we eliminate a judgment, another one forms. The only solution, as in the myth, is to cut the head off the monster; to completely free oneself from the superego. (Avikal E. Costantino, *Tackling the Medusa Within*, Viha Connection, Mill Valley CA, March 2004)

> Every time the individual succeeds in defending against the superego, a certain amount of aggressive energy is liberated and can manifest as anger. This is why anger is frequently experienced simultaneously with the process of defending oneself. In other words, the anger that was directed by the superego toward the ego is now in possession of the ego, to use for whatever purpose it chooses. We have observed that when a person is engaged in the process of disengaging from the superego, she is strengthened and endowed with more energy. In fact, one is strengthened not only by re-owning one's anger, but also and more fundamentally, by integrating the essential aspect of Strength, which is the energetic basis of the emotion of anger.
>
> (A. H. Almaas, *Work on the Superego*, Diamond Books, Berkeley CA, USA, 1992, p. 6)

Defense based on force uses aggressiveness to protect its own space and stop the superego's attack. Once you recognize that you are under attack and you understand the source of the attack, you have only to rebut it, aggressively and with intention, to be successful. You do not need to, in any way, debate the content or merits of the attack itself.

A rebuttal might be turning to your superego and saying, 'Go to hell!' or 'That's it! I've had enough' or 'Mum, I couldn't care less what you think!' Either way, the strength and directness of the response is important. It is also important, for two main reasons, not to get involved in a dialogue with the judge:

It makes no sense to be reasonable about a mechanism that is not rational. It's like arguing with your computer, trying to convince it that it is wrong to use a certain program.

Trying to explain and justify yourself to the superego does nothing more than reaffirm your dependence and the fact that you need its approval. This inadvertently reinforces the judge's power.

When dealing with the superego it is important to respond with firmness and decisiveness and without compromise and justification. You can throw the aggression back to whoever has set it in motion. This will enable you to regain possession of your power without feeling guilty.

Inquiry, meditations and visualizations

Please note: I refer to parts of the body in these practices: the entire belly, for which we use the Japanese term *Hara*; and the center of Hara, three fingers below the belly button inside the body, for which we use the term *Tanden*. Take the time to read Appendix B where you can find the 'Stop!' technique and meditations and visualizations for centering, for grounding and for reconnecting with the Hara center.

1. Explore the ways the superego attacks and manipulates you: what are the situations and what judgments are you aware of?

What are your usual reactions and the tensions associated with them in the body? Delve into the details and let the story come to the surface with its images, memories and understandings. Observe the emotions that surface as a result of this exploration and your attitude towards those emotions. Notice if there's acceptance and/or resistance.

Write down some judgments that arise when you start sentences with 'You are...' and 'You are not...' Find a partner for this inquiry – someone whose role it is to be your superego. After you have written down 4–5 of the most powerful judgments you have towards yourself, give the sheet of paper to your partner. This exercise must be done persistently, using some degree of pressure.

There are two parts to this task: the first task is to let your 'superego' attack you by repeating the judgments you have written using those phrases: 'You are/aren't...' Let your reaction manifest without censoring yourself: you might be angry, furious and start to argue and to counterattack, or you might be sad or hurt and frightened, and you may withdraw, shutting down the senses; you might freeze or you might want to manipulate the superego... let the reaction be as it is.

After 4–5 minutes, both of you should stop and close your eyes and feel what it is like inside: your partner in the role of the superego and you in the role of the attacked.

2. The second task of the exercise is more effective if done standing opposite each other for about 10 minutes. When you are both ready, your partner begins to attack you while you keep your eyes open, keeping your attention on your body and using one of the centering and grounding techniques (outlined in Appendix B).

Your objective is to practice detachment while remaining in contact with yourself and being aware of what happens to you. Continue to look your partner straight in the eyes, remaining silent and turning your attention inside: what do you feel, what do you think and what kind of sensations do you have? If you get distressed, or feel lost or caught up in reaction, practice the 'Stop!' technique (see Appendix B).

Center yourself again. When you feel you are in contact with yourself, start to notice exactly what is happening to you, in your body, your emotions, what thoughts and images you have, and what reactions you notice. Keep your knees relaxed and your feet planted on the ground. Slow the breath. Do this slowly and with attention, while your partner continues to attack you. Let the superego do what it wants; don't get involved, keep your focus on yourself.

At the end of this exercise close your eyes and shake your body for some minutes, visualizing the tensions, the resistance and the reactions falling like big drops on the floor. Stop and take some deep breaths. If you want you can exchange roles. Practicing detachment allows you to stay in touch with yourself, by effectively slowing and steadily distancing yourself from compulsive reactions, and you will begin to have an experience of yourself not as a victim under attack from the judge. The 'detachment' begins to break this automatic identification both with the judge and with the child and, a little at a time, a new sense of self-worth and confidence will begin to manifest based on your ability to remain present and supportive of your growth. The practice of detachment keeps you grounded: you feel that even under attack you can maintain your presence and know where you are and what you feel.

3. Explore your relationship with your rage and aggression. How did your parents face their rage? How did they relate to yours? What memories are associated with aggression in your childhood? Where do you feel the rage in your body, if you feel it? How do you react to the rage of others? Take 15–20 minutes for this exploration.

Your partner plays the role of the superego, attacking you with the list of judgments you have towards yourself. This exploration must be done with a partner, as you did with the 'will' (even better if it is the same person). You will have (as you did for Exercise 2 above) given them your list to read. This exercise is more effective if done standing in front of each other. Keep your eyes open and look the 'superego' in the face while it attacks you, at the same time observing what happens to you. Probably after a while you will feel rage inside and the desire to react; perhaps you feel your body tense and the blood circulating faster. You may feel a desire to raise your voice. Or maybe you don't feel rage at all; on the contrary, you feel confused, drained and without energy.

In both cases, little by little pay attention to the right side of your body, relax your knees and your buttocks, feel your feet on the ground and the floor that supports you. If it helps you, stamp your feet on the ground a few times. Remember that this is a practice to get in touch with your aggressiveness; perhaps this is easy for you or maybe it seems impossible – in any case try to silence the judge.

When you are ready, without hurrying or forcing yourself, tell the superego to go to hell, or to stop it, or whatever expression you think is right. Try different sentences until you find the one that is right for you.

Use your voice and, if you can, let it rise from the belly. Imagine your body becoming fiery red as it expands. You are the lion-heart and David who kills Goliath the giant. Imagine flames coming out of your eyes. Continue for at least 5–6 minutes or, better still, until your partner feels that you have rebuffed them and that it is useless to go on attacking you.

End the exercise by sharing the way you feel, what sensations you feel in your body and... if your judge attacks you inside, tell it to go to hell! If it's difficult for you to defend yourself against the superego using force, ask yourself why you keep thinking that your life isn't worth protecting, and observe the depth of the judgments you have towards force. Explore where they come from.

There is no freedom possible if you are not willing to use all your energy to defend your life. The superego, by holding you in a childish and diminished state, is robbing you, minute by minute, of your life, your joy, your sexuality, your creativeness, your light.

That's why Buddha says that unless you kill your parents you will never become free. Killing the parents means killing the voice of the parent inside you, killing the conscience inside you, dropping these nonsense ideas and starting to live your own life according to your own consciousness. Remember, consciousness has to be more and conscience has to be less. By and by conscience has to disappear completely and pure consciousness has to be lived.

(Osho, *Zen: The Path of Paradox*, Rajneesh Foundation, Pune, India, 1978, vol. 1, ch. 6)

Chapter 7

Self-Image and Space

When working with the superego, and especially when working with those who are just starting out, I continue to stress that the fundamental thing is to learn to be aware of the attacks and manipulations carried out by one's inner judge and the enormous importance of learning to consciously defend ourselves, while at the same time letting go of our infantile reactivity.

Freedom from our inner judge is based on:

A deep understanding that holding on to any denial of the existential slavery in which we live, slavery caused by our infantile relationship with the superego, goes against ourselves, our life, against truth and love.

An unwavering commitment to become aware and to recognize, as many times as possible, when we are under attack from our inner judge and are compulsively reacting in an automatic and unconscious way, as well as when we are projecting our judge externally and attacking the world around us.

Learning to respond consciously by practicing presence and what we call 'non-reactivity', and to use essential will and strength (see Chapter 6) in order to protect the integrity of our lives.

These constitute the foundations, and building them is neither an easy nor painless process: It is one that requires careful consideration, involvement and consistency and it is one that, inevitably, makes us confront our own shadow, our fear of growing, our inclination to avoid taking responsibility for our lives, our yearning to be rescued, the fear of being alone and

5

many, many other manifestations of attachment to our familiar past.

And this, in every case, is only the beginning; there is much more and it involves what I consider to be the most central aspect of the ego–superego dynamic: namely, the way in which we re-create the images of our Self and our world through our inner dialogue CONSTRAINS us to exist (and share) in suffering and separation.

We are all 'superego-dependents'

It is not an easy subject because it includes at least two very 'delicate' aspects:

The first is our attachment to these images due to fear, the survival instinct and a need for security.

The second is the fact that this attachment manifests itself with all the characteristics of an addiction, such as drug abuse, alcohol, pornography, work, TV etc.

When we face these issues, a fragmentation and de-structuring of the personality takes place and, with it, a real crisis of abstinence occurs. This is an intense and formidable stage, and a good internal base of will and strength formed through the initial work on understanding the dynamic between ego and superego is required, along with the practice of conscious defense and the ability to not react mechanically.

It is on this basis that one is able to go through the most important transformation: the conscious dismantling of our self-image and our images of the world that we continually re-create and project on everything around us.

It is a veritable deprogramming and detoxification that involves EVERY dimension of our reality, both internal and external. This deprogramming is fundamentally a process of 'thawing out' the images of ourselves and our reality that have become fixed over time: our frozen personality structure and the resistance to transformation associated to it are key components in our daily suffering and restlessness.

Staying alert to the presence of the judge and learning to respond consciously enables us to train our spiritual muscles, to recognize our capacities and resources, and to be able to draw on them.

Then the moment arrives for putting these resources into action and actively participating in the creation of our daily reality, first of all by dissolving the barriers, the boundaries, which our judgments and prejudices keep on creating in and around us. These exist as inner representations (images) of ourselves, of others, of the world, and have a hazy, uncertain sense of identity at their core.

I'm not beautiful enough, I'm stupid, I have to be the best, if only I was intelligent! I'm a failure, I don't deserve love, I'll never do it... blah, blah, blah... all the things that we keep repeating, all the self-hypnosis that we continue to practice, all the banal, common nonsense that makes up the lens through which we perceive everything, UNKNOWINGLY CREATING AND RE-CREATING REALITY THROUGH THE POWER OF OUR IMAGES AND THE WORDS WE UTTER!

The attachment to our images is the glue that keeps the structure standing and, just like a real fortress, protects us from the mystery and immense aliveness of the present moment.

The fundamental images (self-representations) to be confronted are:

- Images of the body
- Images of the Self
- Images of others

Inquiring into each one of these images and our attachment to them guides us towards an inner experience of Essential Space, through the dissolution of pre-determined boundaries regarded as real and unalterable.

Space opens up

Whenever we become free from the identification with any self-representation, we experience ourselves as being free from the structure patterned by it. This always manifests as some kind of space, as an inner field that feels exactly like empty physical space, but it is a state of consciousness, a pure manifestation of Being.

(A. H. Almaas, *The Point of Existence*, p. 338)

The opening up of Essential Space brings other, more profound identifications to the surface. Those concerning the physical body can be considered to be primary ones and, as such, the most difficult to detect. At the same time, the opening up of Space is necessary in order for our essential qualities to reveal themselves easily and naturally, taking the place of the false images that cover up our nature.

The receptive aspect of compassion helps us to accept our distortions and our attachment to them, unfreezing them simply through love and caring for ourselves; the active aspect of compassion helps us to stay on course, and not to lapse into self-pity or complacency, and, through the evolution of our soul, to see the big picture.

Slowly the images/limitation/separation dissolve and the unpredictable vastness of the here/now is what remains.

Some central points

- We rarely experience reality directly, whether internally or externally. The interior dialogue between the ego and superego that happens on a subconscious level activates a filter (which includes inner representations of ourselves and our world) and it is through this filter that we feel, think and act. By freeing our consciousness from the automatism of reactivity, and learning to be on the alert for attacks by the judge, little by little, it is possible to become more aware of our inner dialogue and therefore recognize how we keep identifying ourselves, whether with the judge or child. This is an enormous step forwards because while, on the one hand, it is quite easy for most people to recognize the presence of the judge and to stop identifying with it, it is much more difficult to let our identification with the (often idealized) child go. The reality is that ego and superego sustain each other in a relationship that is unhealthy and distorted due to complete co-dependency.

- It is only when we recognize and decide to dispense with this co-dependency and our preference for one or the other that the Self-image sustained through this dialogue begins to melt and an otherwise inaccessible vision of reality opens up.

- Our attachment to the judge or the child is therefore the key element to be explored, and the best question to ask ourselves in this case is: 'What am I gaining by attaching myself to my judge or attaching myself to my inner child?' This question should be asked over and over again both in general as well as in specific situations when we realize we have taken sides and we are therefore acting in a limited way, one that is partial and, as such, fundamentally not in line with the truth.

- This process inevitably brings about the destruction of our Self-image, which means that habitual reference points for our identity – physical, emotional and mental – tend to disappear or become more transparent and this radically changes the perception of our inner space. In this phase, an active and dynamic inquiry will provide us with the greatest support, especially when carried out with the help of someone who has already gone through the process or is familiar with it.

Not only does space correct the distortion of body-image and dissolve the psychological boundaries of the self-image, it ultimately dissolves the self-image as a rigid structure bounding experience. This provides a hint regarding the ontological truth about self-image. Since we see that space makes the body-image objective and realistic, i.e., correcting it according to objective reality, we can assume that it also corrects the self-image according to objective reality. That is, ontologically, self-image is simply boundaries frozen in space, frozen by their cathexis [concentration of psychic energy on a single goal – author's note] with libidinal energy. When the cathexis is undone, the boundaries dissolve into empty space, which is what actually exists as the nature of the mind. Therefore, we can say that pursuing the psychodynamic understanding of the self-image all the way to the end will leave us with, among other things, a real and objective body-image and the experience of mind as open space.

(A. H. Almaas, *The Void*, p. 52)

Consciously dismantling one's own image not only requires great care and commitment but above all, COMPASSION: compassion for ourselves and the world that we have created and that, in a narcissistic way, we continue to create. This radical compassion is what enables us to heal the wounds that are hidden under the frozen images from our past; it helps us look at the false masks that we wear and insist on protecting. It is compassion which enables us to recognize and sense our isolation, our fear of not being able to cope, our resignation as well as our real and sincere need for others.

Inquiry, meditations and visualizations

1. Explore your loop of attack/reaction in the relationship between your coercive side (the superego) and the child within you. Choose a specific aspect from your life (for

example, your work or a personal relationship or your relationship with money, success, sexuality, etc.) and explore how the judge attacks and manipulates you, through what judgments, how it does this, by creating pressure, a sense of guilt, how it attacks your values and how the child reacts to these attacks. When you are involved in this inner dynamic and identifying with it, what is your experience of space? How do you perceive it – is it open, expansive, welcoming, or is it suffocating and tight, like a vice?

2. Once again, in a situation of attack/reaction, now practice conscious defense, using presence and will as outlined in the preceding chapters. Observe the attack/reaction dynamic without judging it, without making negative or positive evaluations; don't get involved, but rather exert your will and remain as an observer. Note any physical symptoms, emotional associations, and simply be present with what is happening, without changing anything. Observe, sense what is taking place and note whether your perception of your inner space changes in any way.

Chapter 8

The Gossip Swamp

Gossip in itself is neither good nor bad and it is certainly not my intention to judge an activity which is evidently very widespread and sustained in diverse ways in our culture; at the same time, if we stop to take an honest look at gossip it is likewise simple to see that when it becomes a compulsive habit, it very quickly turns into a swamp in which it is easy to get stuck. Let's try and understand then the purpose for gossip, and how tittle-tattling helps us, what space it creates in and around us, and, above all, what is behind it. But first, a story.

In ancient Greece, Socrates was held in high regard for his wisdom and integrity.

One day one of his colleagues came to him all excited and out of breath saying, 'Socrates, do you know what I've just heard about Diogenes?'

'Wait a moment,' replied Socrates. 'Before you tell me, I want you to take a little test, the one with three filters.'

'Three filters?' remarked the other.

'Exactly,' continued Socrates. 'Before telling me about Diogenes let's take a moment to filter what you want to tell me. The first filter is Truth; are you absolutely sure that what you intend to tell me is the truth?'

'No,' his colleague replied. 'In reality I've only heard other people talking about it.'

'OK,' said Socrates. 'Then you don't know for sure whether it's true or not. Let's try the second filter: the filter of Kindness. Is what you're going to tell me about Diogenes something kind?'

'No, on the contrary...'

'So then,' continued Socrates, 'you want to tell me something about Diogenes that's negative, perhaps offensive, even though you don't know whether it's true?'

The man got to his feet blushing, somewhat embarrassed, and Socrates continued, 'Maybe you can still pass the test because there is a third filter: the filter of Usefulness. Is what you want to tell me about Diogenes useful? Will it help me in some way?'

'No, I don't think so.'

'Fine,' concluded Socrates. 'If it isn't true, good or useful, what's the point of telling me or anyone else?'

What do I achieve by gossiping?

Gossip has several functions:

- The first one is fundamentally cathartic. Through gossip (which is a particularly charged and energetic form of judgment) the mental pressure and emotions generated by my inner relationship with my judge can be released. The burden of internal aggression with which my inner judge attacks me with the goal of maintaining the status quo at all costs is deflected externally. This enables my judge to conceal the power that it exerts on me and regulate my vital energy, keeping things that are deemed to be dangerous or unacceptable in the unconscious. Expressing negative opinions, judgments, devaluating others, or simply turning my attention to other people, I can offload energy that has accumulated internally and that could otherwise lead to tension and anxiety.

  Speaking can be of many kinds. One kind of speaking is that which has no concern at all with your listener. In this case speaking is just your disease: you speak because you cannot remain quiet, because there is much noise and turbulence going on in your head. By speaking you become light ... so your speaking is just a catharsis. This is how we are all speaking, because we feel restless if we don't speak. In speaking the restlessness gets released. This is why, once you have chattered enough, you become light, and then you go home and have a good night's sleep. The day you do not get enough chance to gossip you will have trouble sleeping that night, because when you are not able to gossip with the other you will have to gossip with yourself. So lying in your bed you will be talking to yourself. For you, speaking is a disease, a compulsion. What you are speaking about does not concern you. It is also a question whether you are speaking to do good or harm to anybody. You speak because you cannot stop yourself from speaking ... There is a restlessness within, and that restlessness is released through talking.

(Osho, *Nowhere To Go But In*, Chapter 13, online library, www.osho.com)

- Attacking someone or something that is external unconsciously allies me with my inner judge and, temporarily, I don't feel the friction of the internal conflict between the parents and child within. I feel like I'm in control, that I know what is right; I feel sure of having concrete information and making true appraisals.

- It is also a way to entertain oneself, to create a show in which the actors are other people and I am the public and the critic. And in this apparently objective position I create alliances with the other members of the public, creating a clan element based on a common standpoint. The weakness of me turns into the power of us.

What is behind gossip?

When we begin to look at the mechanics of gossip it becomes clear that gossip is simply a habitual, unconscious way of projecting ourselves externally, where the most immediate effect is of getting out of oneself so that we can avoid recognizing, and above all intimately feeling, what, in a specific situation, affects us, what something has to do with us, how we feel about it, what our judgments are, our prejudices, our values, the effects that that specific relationship has on us. In brief, gossip enables us to avoid our own feelings and possible vulnerabilities.

It is a way of deflecting negative judgments that my judge makes about me, and repressed material that is hidden in my unconscious, and attaching it to someone else, thereby avoiding feeling the pain of self-repression. It is a way of diverting the self-hatred that lies hidden beneath a method of self-defense based on the ongoing control, aggression and the manipulation of my instincts, feelings and needs by the superego.

Gossip is fundamentally a release valve and a form of energy regulation; it is completely in the hands of the inner judge and used for hiding its presence and for not feeling an inner current of violence.

Projection, of which gossip is often a widespread form, allows us to avoid feeling the cage we live in, its limits, the pressure and abuse to which we are subjected daily by our structure of control and survival. And, what is more, projection helps us to feel GOOD AND RIGHT, better than others; gossip is one of the most usual ways through which we raise ourselves and belittle others.

How then can we intervene in this compulsive mechanism that, if kept unconscious, inevitably produces negative effects on our relationships?

As always, the first step is to recognize that the mechanism exists in our daily lives, becoming aware of the ways in which it manifests itself and removing any judgments we have in this respect, recognizing how judgment itself stops us from truly understanding the characteristics of the mechanism, its functions and its effects. To remove the judgment I have to first of all recognize what judgments I have, how they manifest or stay hidden. Inquiry is the way forward.

Inquiry, meditations and visualizations

1. Am I addicted to gossip? Do I recognize the presence of this habit in my life, and if so, in which situations in particular? Am I aware of why I gossip or not? Is it an automatic reaction? How do I feel when I gossip, while I'm doing it and afterwards? Can I recognize particular physical symptoms and specific, associated emotions?

2. Do I have opinions on gossiping? What are they? How do I react when I find out that other people are talking about me behind my back? What are the physical symptoms, emotions and thoughts – reactions that rise to the surface in this case?

3. If I let go of the judgments I hold regarding gossiping, what purpose does this mechanism have in my life? Is it a defense mechanism? If so, what does it defend me from?

4. How can I tell the difference between when my gossip doesn't contain destructive energy and when it does? What are my inner feelings in both these cases?

5. What effects does gossiping have on my relationships?

6. What type of atmosphere is created with the person/people I am with when gossiping becomes the main form of our communication?

7. How can I become aware of this mechanism? What commitment can I make to myself in the direction of being more aware?

The fourth filter

There is another filter that has always worked for me; it is a filter of the heart and it reflects the most ancient principle of love: Do unto others what you would like to be done to you.

If you find you're unsure about something you're about to say about another person; if you recognize the things I have said previously at least in some part and you understand that gossiping is a way of escaping from yourself and for offloading your tensions onto the world; if you can recognize potential destructiveness in what you are about to say, then take one more step and use the fourth filter.

You will begin to be, in the flesh, the transformation that you might want to see around you.

Chapter 9

Freedom from Guilt

There is no way that we can be free from guilt as long as we believe we are the personality's lesser ego. Whenever we keep identifying with a fundamental lie – the mask of what I believe I am, learnt through conditioning and protected by superego activity – we remain in a constant state of self-deceit and self-conceit. In this state of subversion from our Natural State – a state of Wholeness and Integrity – we keep dividing ourselves and reality between good and bad, allowed and not allowed, condemned and valued. In this state of disconnection we are enslaved by our past and in a permanent position of having to protect the status quo, far removed from authenticity and in an almost constant state of fragmentation.

This fragmentation implies suffering, and the suffering creates friction at the very core of our sense of identity, as well as a fundamental addiction.

We are addicted to suffering because we have the need to assuage our guilt with suffering – with the destruction of ourselves and others through various subtle and not-so-subtle means. And underneath all our suffering there exists this insatiable need to be right, to be self-righteous, because the egological self survives by being right in procuring and securing meaning in life.

Guilt arises as the attempt at self-righteousness in the face of the recognition that we have done something wrong or committed sin. Guilt arises when we try to be right in the face of the recognition that we are wrong. There is nothing that gives us the sense of self-righteousness more than the sense of guilt, because we can thereby simultaneously humble ourselves so lowly as to be sinners and elevate ourselves so highly as to be the sole judge and punisher of our sins – the role normally reserved only for God.

(Yasuhiko Genku Kimura, *'Project Beauty and Freedom from Fear and Guilt'*, VIA, vol. 2, no. 3/4)

What wrong have we done? What sin have we committed? Exactly what is this gnawing feeling that never leaves us; the feeling that we are somehow out of place, not truly ourselves, incomplete? If we look within with openness and honesty we are bound to recognize that day after day we keep betraying ourselves. We bend to fit, we hide to adapt; we separate ourselves from what is true, from what our heart whispers, our guts warm to and our mind dreams in its glorious visions; and we pretend to be that small, shrunken shape that we call 'me'. **The only sin we have committed is forgetting who we really are; self-forgetfulness is the original sin.**

And day after day, as we try to keep booting up new survival programs, holding false images of ourselves and the world in order to keep it somehow together, we find ourselves caught between a rock and a hard place: We need suffering to relieve our guilt and we need guilt to justify our suffering; the basic fuel of the false identity.

In order to experience the only guilt that's of value – the spiritual one, the one that involves a longing to be true to ourselves – we need to learn to rid ourselves of the guilt generated by our infantile relationship with our superego. To do this it is helpful to explore some basic functions of egoic, mundane guilt in order to gain insight. We can start this journey just by asking ourselves some fundamental questions: Why do we need to feel guilty? What do we achieve through self-punishment?

Guilt as defense

Most people believe guilt is simply an emotion. However, guilt is a much more complex phenomenon as it involves thought patterns, beliefs, concepts, emotions and physical sensations. Depending on the structure of our personality, we will have a particular way of experiencing guilt: for some people it is fundamentally a mental activity, a run of thoughts and contrasting points of view; for others it is a feeling of being crushed, associated with despair, helplessness, unworthiness; for others it is a heavy mantel that freezes the body, either numbing it or making it hyperactive and restless... In trying to experientially understand the psychodynamic of guilt we have to explore and open ourselves up to other dimensions, moving away from our well-trodden path of guilt. As we do that we will discover very personal symptoms that alert us to the emergence of guilt; a whole spectrum of mental, emotional and physical aspects.

In this chapter I want to point towards an aspect of guilt that is most often left behind or altogether denied: guilt as a defense mechanism.

Guilt as a defense mechanism has three fundamental goals:

- To shift the subject's attention from the experience of the present moment – with all its associated feelings and sensations – to the inner dialogue, essentially re-enacting the familiar relationship between the coercive agency (internalized parents) and the child.
- The fundamental attempt to regain innocence and righteousness through self-punishment.
- The avoidance of taking responsibility for whatever event has caused the feeling of wrongness.

From feeling/attention to thinking/imagination

The imperative in this case is: Move away from the present!

This is best done by moving one's attention away from the

sensory and emotional aspects of the experience in hand at that moment.

You might have noticed how guilt is initially experienced as an often overwhelming constellation of many different sensory and emotional elements and how, in the blink of an eye, to avoid the feeling of 'not being in control', our tendency is to break connection with the sensory and emotional part of the experience and get more and more involved with the mental. The energetic movement is from down to up, from feeling/sensation to thinking/imagination; in a way, guilt becomes disembodied and the person ends up locked into the psychological, the conceptual, the inner dialogue between ego and superego; in the 'shoulds' and 'shouldn'ts', in schemes aimed at adjusting the mistake or hiding it, offsetting it, and so on. Through this process we disconnect from guilt as an aspect of what we are experiencing in the present and, instead, identify with it as an abstract category defined by our past. We identify with a familiar self-image that has a familiar experience of guilt and uses familiar tools for dealing with it. And, in this way, even through guilt we can reinforce the status quo.

Guilt as restoration of self-righteousness

By judging and punishing oneself, as Kimura pointed out in the previous quote, we are assuming the role of God, as we are defining right and wrong, judging, inflicting punishment, absolving ourselves and offering redemption, and, finally, restoring righteousness. At the end of the guilt process we may well feel like we are innocent again and among the cohorts of the righteous ones. As we reposition ourselves in the RIGHT, our world re-asserts its precarious balance, and all the boundaries and values reappear, clear and well cut, beyond doubt, beyond questioning. Guilt lets us forget the uncertainty of a morality we have been forced to eat, digest and make our own. Egotistical self-reproach helps us to forget that we are individuals and takes us back into the comforting embrace of mediocrity.

Guilt and responsibility

Lastly, guilt as a defense mechanism enables us to avoid growing up and facing up to our habit of betraying the truth. We can lie to ourselves, we can lie to others. We can justify our unwillingness to face the consequences of the truth and the risk of being authentic: We can keep on hiding behind the mask – its conventions, its unspoken emotional contracts – and we can choose not to grow up, not to take responsibility for our shortcomings and mistakes. It is like when a little child has broken something and then, when asked if he did it, innocently says, 'No, it just fell and broke!' This is an innocent and somewhat sweet disposition in little children but it is certainly a different matter altogether in supposed adults. Deviating from, or denying responsibility is a little game we all play, as we complain, bitch, pout, blame, rag, shunning what it has to do with us in any way we can and steering clear of why we act that way. By avoiding responsibility for whatever the truth is with regards to a particular event, we keep ourselves confined to habitual patterns built in the past: We might feel guilty and go through the process of self-judgment and self-punishment, and in such a way make ourselves feel worthy again but, by doing this, we pay the price of remaining small and impotent in the face of change.

Inquiry, meditations and visualizations

1. Explore the need to feel guilty. What do you achieve through self-punishment? What is the function of guilt in your life? What happens in your body as you start contemplating these questions? What are the feelings that emerge?
2. What place does guilt have in your life? In what parts of your life can you recognize the presence of guilt and what are the mechanics of the experience of guilt? How do you feel about it?

3. Explore the need and compulsion to be right. Where does it manifest most significantly in your daily life? How do you feel in those situations – what are the physical, emotional and mental symptoms you are aware of?

4. How does guilt affect your love relationships?

5. Is habitual lying and finding excuses something that you can see happening to you in day-to-day life? If yes, what are the situations? How do you feel when you avoid taking responsibility? How do you feel afterwards?

Part 3

Being Yourself

Chapter 10

The Inner Judge and Sexuality

Every infant has a powerful relationship to its sensual self. It has a libido or, at least, libidinal energy which is a fundamental component of the infant's vitality. This energy influences the way a baby or infant perceives itself and the reality surrounding it. We can say that every experience of the child is associated with sensuality.

One of the fundamental elements in the formation of the superego is the control and repression of sexual instincts. So, it is the sexual impulses of the child that often cause the strongest reactions from the parents and are, often, the major impulses repressed by the parents.

Freud's classic theory sees the formation of the fundamental components of the superego in internalization, especially of the parent of the same sex, and of their reactions and creation of taboos in the oedipal phase of the child's development.

The oedipal phase (4 or 5 years of age) sees little boys naturally experiencing an often overwhelming sexual attraction towards their mother; the oedipal phase sees little girls falling in love with their father. At the same time, the child develops aggressive and competitive tendencies towards the parent of the same sex.

If, in this phase, the child is understood, accepted and supported by parents and is given positive feedback about the development and transformation of their sexuality (mother and father being the first external 'objects of desire'), the child won't feel attacked and rejected but rather appreciated and acknowledged and will, more than likely, be able to integrate this phase of development in a healthy way.

This, unfortunately, is not the most widespread reality. In most cases the parents feel threatened by the open sexuality and competitiveness of their child and they respond in an inadequate (and ignorant) way. They do this by unconsciously transferring to the child their own inner dynamics of fear, control and repression.

Natural curiosity is destroyed

Every child has a natural curiosity and an immense desire to sense itself and explore the world around, and what is it closer to than its own body? What is more miraculous than all the sensations that arise moment after moment by seeing, smelling, tasting and touching? So the child happily discovers its own body through all its senses with joy and abandon. If you look at a little one, you can easily see the wonderment and innocence of that exploration.

And yet every child becomes the object of reproach, cold stares, cutting words, or worse, when he is touching the genitals. The innocence of pleasurable discovery is interrupted by condemnation. In the developing personality of the child an imprint starts forming, an association between sexual exploration and wrongness; between delighting in one's own body and guilt.

This association will later on cripple the adult, bringing inhibition and self-judgment, lack of presence and automatism in lovemaking. And will transform one of the simplest and most natural life experiences into something overcharged and distorted, emotionally and mentally. The genitals are the natural center of sexuality. If the natural discovery of the genitals is interrupted or distorted by parental interference, then later expressions of sexuality will be determined by mental images and concepts rather than by feelings and sensations.

Acceptance or rejection of sexual drives

The parents' reactions to the developing libido of their child are fundamental in determining how the future adult perceives, experiences and expresses sexuality.

In particular, what are called castration and performance anxieties are shaped by the parents' reactions to the child in the oedipal phase. Parents who have the capacity to respond in a loving and healthy way to the child's curiosity and manifesting of sexual desires will be able to support the natural growth of the self and the integration of deep unconscious impulses. They will create an empathic bond with the child that will make the child feel welcome and supported, accepted and recognized in their expressions of adoration and innocent competition.

In fact, at that stage Mother and Father are the embodied representations of the Goddess and God. They are the first and ultimate objects of desire and, to the developing genital passion of the child, nothing is more desirable, valuable or worth dying for. It is not difficult then to understand how the imprint that the child receives in that period will shape the core of its sexual identity and condition all future relationships.

When parents react with contempt, disgust, rejection, withdrawal or preoccupation, they implant those seeds in the forming psyche of the child, creating the ground of future fears of rejection, self-mistrust and guilt.

In the same way, the incapacity or unwillingness of the parents to deal with the child might manifest as absence of direction or avoidance. In this situation the child is left alone with confusion and lack of direction or knowing.

Worse still, the parents might take a road of ambivalence or excessive permissiveness that might give the child the suggestion that they can 'win' the mother or the father at any time. This will completely destabilize the natural position of the child in the family environment.

An essential part of our inner coercive formation, therefore, is generated by the rejection of our sexual drives from one or both our parents. We also have the need to internalize the judgments, the criticisms and the moral values of that parent in order to ensure and maintain their love. Our superego then takes on those same values, those same judgments, and attacks us every time our sexuality manifests itself in forms that our superego considers 'inappropriate'.

The most immediate manifestation of this repressive activity of the superego is a particular form of anxiety commonly called 'castration anxiety'. It manifests in men and in women and, even though the form for each gender is different, there is a common basic component: **the sensation of not having what we need in order to face the situations that life offers us.**

This anxiety may have sexual origins, but it is pervasive. It expands to include anxiety about our overall capacity to be vital, powerful and have the resources we need. The superego attacks our manhood and femininity, our ability to love, our ability to feel and to give pleasure, our ability to have close relationships, to be present and to support ourselves and others, our creativity and our ability to play on the world's stage.

Effects of castration anxiety

The most common effect of castration anxiety is a deep mistrust of our own abilities and a fear of our sexuality and vitality. Our libidinal power becomes a monster, our inner monster – the wild beast with unacceptable lustful drives and primitive desires that must be tamed and hidden.

The fear of this beast – shrouded in darkness and ready to possess us – pulses under our skin, in our muscles and in our imagination. It resides together with the desire, unmentioned and unmentionable, of a complete and spontaneous sexuality. Our every action and plan, almost everything that deals with sexuality – a desire, a fantasy, a touch, a smile – must go through the scrutiny and approval of the superego.

When we fear our libidinal power, we are isolated from the power of life itself; the natural connection between the Individual Self and the Universe is cut, denied, forgotten.

And the small dictator inside us – the superego – reinforces, in every way, our dependency and need for obedience and assurance. It also, most distressingly, imbues us with mistrust in our ability to grow and take life into our own hands.

The Japanese philosopher, Yasuhiko Kimura, writing about the particular fear of our libidinal power, says:

Fearful people are easy to manipulate and exploit. For this reason, throughout history, the power structures of the world have used psychological manipulations to make the populace fearful and dependent. For instance, consider the association of sex with the notion of sin: when the natural desire and act of sex is condemned as sinful from the beginning of life, people tend to disconnect themselves from the natural thrust of life, which belongs to the Self of the universe. Disconnected from the Self of the universe, they become fearful. Fearful people do not tend to develop genuine self-autonomy; instead, they become dependent upon external authority. Once people become fearful and dependent, the power structures, posing as their protectors or saviors, can easily exploit them. Fearful people do not possess the necessary confidence to think or act independently, and thus become followers of external authorities. For them, as Helen Keller put it, life is not a daring adventure but a constant search for security and assurance.

(Yasuhiko Genku Kimura, *'Project Beauty and Freedom from Fear and Guilt'*, *VIA*, vol. 2, no. 3/4, USA, 2004, p. 6)

Guilt and shame

The most evident symptoms we have seen of the superego's presence, of being under attack, are feelings of guilt and shame.

These are even more evident to us, when we consider our repressed sexuality.

Sexual desire has been inextricably linked to the concept of sin and evil mostly through religious and family conditioning. Guilt and shame are the price we pay for our 'impure' thoughts and actions. And, through self-judgment and guilt, we punish ourselves for having sinned and therefore created evil. Kimura again:

> When we sentence ourselves to be guilty, we self-righteously judge and punish ourselves for our sin. When we project or extend our own guilt to others, we then judge and punish them. Virtually all of our destructive tendencies or activities toward ourselves and others – including chronic addiction, chronic illness, chronic war and chronic social dysfunction – stem from the subversive nature inherent in the psycho-dynamics of guilt. Usually quietly but sometimes violently and almost always non consciously, we punish and destroy our self, our health, and our world in order to assuage and thereby justify our guilt.'
> (Ibid, p. 8)

In bowing to the values and prejudices of the superego – to the fears and prejudices of our parents and society – we judge ourselves. In doing so, we administer the punishment, castrating our vital force and destroying our passion.

The consequences are all too familiar: rejection of our sexuality and of our body; neurotic attempts to manipulate it and make it 'the perfect body', the inability to discover its potential and to enjoy it fully; insecurity and anxiety about our sexual behavior and performance; compulsive sexuality, deviations and perversions, secrecy...

For as long as we fail to understand the fundamental nature of these feelings of guilt and shame and their relationship with the superego, our access to happiness, health, *joie de vivre* and peace will remain blocked, and the fundamental source of our vitality will continue to escape us.

This is what we have taken on, and is what we live. But perhaps even more destructively, this is what we inadvertently give to our children.

Libidinal energy is life force

The libidinal impulse is not only sexual. It involves all our vital forces and our ability to feel alive and ready for the adventure, for discovery, for risk. Castration is, mostly, the deep conviction that it isn't worth continuing to try, that there is no possibility of success and satisfaction; that our infantile or adolescent dreams of great and bright horizons – those intense passions and desires – must all be left behind, swept under layers of frustration, deprivation and desperation.

When the libidinal drive is controlled, sabotaged, diminished or even extinguished by the superego and the fear it produces, what we are left with is reactivity, disillusion and rage. We have lost the vital breath of our soul and evolutionary process.

When we understand clearly the depth of this betrayal – how powerfully it works to our detriment day after day, in the name of loyalty to our judge – then we start to take responsibility for changing this dynamic of self-repression. Then, we can begin to harness the rage that until now we have turned against ourselves and the people around us. We can then use it to counter the superego.

In this stage of working on oneself, the ego turns against the superego, instead of against the id or the other repressed parts of the soul. We mentioned before that the superego uses the energy of aggression against the ego, at this stage this aggression is turned outward against the superego. Besides dealing with the superego effectively, the ego now has access to energy which it can use to deal with the external world. Previously, this energy was used to defend against the life force; now it can be used in its service. Not only is the energy of aggression retrieved for the service of life, but its distortion is eliminated in the process. The individual not only learns to use this energy for defending herself, but also re-owns her essential strength.

As we have seen, the superego is nothing but the internalized coercive agencies that were once external forces. So dealing with one's own superego goes hand in hand with dealing with all coercive agencies in the environment, especially the superego of others. In the process, the individual learns how to deal with his environment efficiently, and his aggression becomes used for life, instinctual and essential, as is appropriate. Dealing with one's own mind, then, and dealing with the external world are part of the same process.

(A. H. Almaas, *Work on the Superego*, Diamond Books, Berkeley CA, USA, 1992, p. 6)

Regaining the sanctity of life

When we regain possession of our aggression and learn to consciously direct it in defense of existence, we demonstrate – through action and presence – an understanding of the sanctity of everything that lives, starting with ourselves. Our body, our emotions, our awareness, our every action, becomes sacred and worthy of attention, care and reverence.

We no longer need an inner entity that continually attacks and manipulates us, dictating the terms of our existence. We grow up, and leave behind the habitual and ritualistic conscience, and replace it with a lively and spontaneous consciousness capable of responding creatively and originally to every situation.

Inquiry, meditations and visualizations

1. Explore the relationship with your body. This self-inquiry is very effective if done alone and in front of a mirror. You will need time to write in your notebook. Look at your reflection for a while and then, closing your eyes, observe what happens inside. Notice:

a. all the judgments that surface (even the most absurd ones).

b. the feelings in your body in relation to those judgments. Where is the tension? Have you lost feeling in some parts of your body? Have they become less sensitive?

c. the kinds of emotions that appear. Are you feeling rage? Frustration? Cynicism? Disgust? Anything else? Notice whether the memories of your childhood that might float to the surface are linked to the relationship with your body or to your parents' attitude to your body. Observe your attitude towards those judgments: where and what you agree with, and where and what you disagree with. Observe where there is shame and where there is guilt. Notice if an inner debate begins between the superego and the ego; if the child who defends themselves from attacks is there; and how you identify with one or the other.

2. Explore your relationship with sexuality. This exploration can be done alone, writing in your notebook, or – and this is certainly more powerful – with a friend, even better if they are willing to do it in turn. Allow 20–30 minutes per person and explore the themes of sexuality and how it was lived, expressed, rejected or hidden in your family.

Try to identify and define some judgments and prejudices – open or hidden – that were present in your family environment in relation to sexuality. You may remember statements like: 'Men want only one thing', 'Sex is a duty for women', 'Masturbating causes blindness', 'Enjoying sex is for whores', 'Don't speak about sex'... and so on. Now explore your sexual life and how you feel in relation to it.

Observe the ways in which your family's story and the conditioning received manifests in your life at present. Explore your desires and drives and the way you live them or repress them. What judgments do you have in respect to them and what happens in your body when you observe, recognize and communicate them?

3. Explore how the superego attacks your sexuality. Try to be as specific and precise as possible: identify particular situations and judgments. What are the symptoms of the attacks: the feelings in your body, your emotions, your internal reactions to others? Observe if there is a repetitive pattern that you recognize and have to confront again and again. Notice what happens in your body when you write or communicate what you find.

4. This is a visualization and breathing exercise that should take 15–20 minutes. Make notes of all your experiences in doing this exercise. Lie on your back and close your eyes. Let the breath slow down and the body relax. Imagine the thoughts and anxieties falling like drops on the floor or on a mattress, and your body expanding with every drop that falls. Take your focus to the genital area and be aware of your feelings without changing any of them. Maybe you find 'nothing' and perhaps there are no feelings, as if there weren't any genitals, or maybe there is a hole, a sense of emptiness. Maybe there are very unclear feelings, as if the genitals were transparent. Can you feel aliveness there? Is there a sense of presence?

Simply observe your experience in this moment, and whether your superego attacks you, saying that it should be different. Defend yourself against the attack if necessary. Stay with the feelings and images that come up. Don't force yourself in any way to be different. Pay attention to any changes in feelings, of the emotions and images.

Become aware of the physical aspects of your experience: temperature, dimension, density, form, energy levels, and so on. After a while, start to visualize your inspiration of breath as a fluid that enters your body through your genitals, arriving at the top of the head and leaving again through the genitals with the exhalation.

Before you stand up, let the visualization go, open your eyes and remain lying without doing anything for a couple of minutes. Turn onto your left side and, helping yourself with your arms, sit up.

Chapter 11

The Inner Judge in Personal Relationships

All relationships are influenced by our inner dynamic with the superego. The level of influence depends on the degree of awareness we have about that dynamic. Most commonly, we each project our own inner judge onto other people, groups of people, on God and, especially, on the people we love.

Loving relationships are therefore the best ground for observing the way our inner judge attacks us and others.

Our deepest self-judgments arise wherever there is a strong emotional involvement, attachment, conscious and unconscious bonds based on survival, complex webs of personal stories, expectations, common dreams and so on. This is also where we create our judgments towards friends, spouses, partners, children and so on.

It is sometimes astounding how precisely the people around us tend to embody our inner judge and confront us with judgments that reflect exactly those we have toward ourselves. We also do the same for them. Whether we admit it or not, often it's the people closest to us who are able to touch our trigger points in a particularly effective way.

This reciprocal judging is probably one of the principal causes of conflict and suffering in a relationship, yet it is also a great opportunity to understand how we project our superego to the outside, and to see how we attack others and, unconsciously, attract attacks from others.

If we look at our interpersonal conflicts from a different perspective – one which includes understanding of the presence of the superego and its negative effects – then it is not difficult to understand that most of the external conflicts are the reflection of unresolved internal conflicts between the judge and the inner child, who continues to react in a mechanical way.

Identification with judge and child

As we have described in previous chapters, this model of behavior embodies the movement of alternating identification with the judge attacking us, and then with the child who tries to avoid the attack by activating habitual defenses.

Like a pendulum, we shift, minute after minute, from being our own executioner (identification with the judge) to being the victim (identification with the child). The same thing happens in intimate relationships, where sometimes we attack the other person, becoming their superego, and sometimes we react to an attack by taking the role of the victim.

Unconscious defenses

However, when we act and react, we invariably invoke an unconscious defense mechanism. That is part of our response to attack. By projecting our superego onto the other, we activate a defense mechanism that allows us to maintain the dynamic with our judge in the unconscious by disowning it. When we are the victims of attacks from the other, we don't have to feel the attack internally and we can, instead, put up our defenses against an external enemy. Conversely, by attacking the other with our criticisms, opinions and prejudices, we avoid thinking about (or feeling) the pain that those same criticisms, opinions and prejudices cause when directed at us.

When two people are relating, it is not only their conscious egos that are involved but also their superegos. The superego is present in the majority of cases in varying degrees and intensities. When a person is rejecting or accepting according to certain values, it is the superego that is at work. When a person is envious, jealous, afraid, etc., it is frequently the

result of the prejudices of his superego.
(A. H. Almaas, *Work on the Superego*, Diamond Books, Berkeley CA, USA, 1992, pp. 8, 9)

Modern psychology posits the view, as do Almaas and many spiritual teachers, that most of our relationships are not, in essence, relations between individuals but between their superegos.

Seeing things as they really are

Rarely do we truly see and hear the people around us. Rather, we see and hear what our superego interprets about the people around us, through its baggage of judgments and prejudices.

We see through 'colored glasses' that filter the information that reaches us; we interpret the world and people according to criteria defined by the structure of our values, standards, opinions, positions and prejudices. Our perception is not direct and immediate. It is continually filtered by our conditioning.

In intimate relations particularly, this often operates through a mechanism known as 'transference'. Transference, in this context, is an unconscious projection of the ideas about or feelings for one of our parents onto the person we love. Since the superego is the internalization of our parents, we end up projecting our superego onto the person we love. And, sadly but invariably, the relationship becomes trapped in a web of delusions, wounds, resentment, complaints and blame.

We can say that the less free a person is from his superego, the more his relationships are determined by it – not only in the choice of partners but also in what transpires in the relationship. If the superegos complement each other, we have a stable relationship. But it is stable only as long as there is no growth or change. It is asserted here that in the majority of cases, stable relationships are ones in which the two superegos can live together without too much friction. In other words, they are superego relationships and not real ones. In fact often the individuals involved dislike each other but they still stay together because of the dominance of their superegos. This is the situation when relationships are based on dependency and insecurity. In other cases, the couple cannot stay together although they love each other, because the superegos don't get along. This explains those cases in which a couple experiences difficulty when their two sets of parents don't get along; because their superegos, as a result, cannot get along. So a couple can spend their whole life together but never really come into close contact because it is the superegos that are in relationship.

(Ibid, p. 9)

Creating real relationships

What we need, in order to have real relationships, is to rid ourselves of the expectation that the person we love is compatible with the criteria and prejudices of our parents, or that our partner behaves so as to satisfy these criteria. Accordingly we will be able to see, feel and appreciate the other in their individuality and originality.

To do this, we need to resolve, or at least to tackle, the relationship with our superego so that our choice of partner is not unconsciously influenced from the beginning, by our projection of either father or mother.

This resolution of the relationship with the superego is not a question of only having the will to look inside us and to understand our conditioning, but of also assuming responsibility, acting with awareness, defending ourselves consciously from our superego's attacks, recognizing the situations in which we project it onto the other, and finding concrete ways to demolish judgments and prejudices. It is those judgments that make our affection and our love conditional.

Acknowledging that the conditions we propose to others are our superego's and our parents', is not an easy thing; it means assuming responsibility completely for our life. It means stopping the blaming of others as the cause of our suffering, frustration and delusion.

It means also recognizing that love is true love only if it is unconditional, that is, free of the superego.

What does love feel like?
Do you remember the exhilarating moments at the beginning of love, in the first days, in the first months? Do you remember the sensation of expansion and lightness, the power of passion and the excitement of the senses? Do you remember the dreams and the absence of time when you are with your loved one? Remember the curiosity and wonder?

Certainly, this is an intoxicating state and there will be lots of elements that can't last. What is also operating is the projection of our dreams that ensures we are not truly in touch with the other's authentic self.

In the first flush of love there is though, most commonly, also the presence of unconditional love which allows us to hold off from measuring the other with the superego's ruler. We don't want the other in the likeness of father or mother.

What betrays love?
Just as these conditions that the superego has given us limit the experience of ourselves and keep us confined in familiar territories, so too do these conditions destroy our intimate relationships and our love.

If we want to be seen, understood and recognized, we must begin to see how we betray ourselves by re-creating, time after time, conditional love towards ourselves; responses where we reject and condemn ourselves. We need to be aware that with those same judgments and actions, we condemn and reject the people we love.

Love allows freedom; not only allows, but strengthens freedom. And anything that destroys freedom is not love. It must be something else. Love and freedom go together, they are two wings of the same bird. Whenever you see that your love is going against your freedom, then you are doing something else in the name of love.

Let this be your criterion: freedom is the criterion; love gives you freedom, makes you free, liberates you. And once you are totally yourself, you feel grateful to the person who has helped you. That gratefulness is almost religious. You feel in the other person something divine. He has made you free, or she has made you free, and love has not become a possessiveness...

If you are in love, the love I am talking about, your very love will help the other to be integrated. Your very love will become a cementing force for the other. In your love the other will come together, because your love will give freedom; and under the shade of your love, under the protection of your love, the other will start growing.

All growth needs love – but unconditional love. If love has conditions then growth cannot be total, because those conditions will come in the way. Love unconditionally.

(Osho, *The Search*, Rajneesh Foundation, Pune, India, 1977, ch. 6)

Growing up together

Where and how does unconditional love start? The 'where' is here. This, of course, rests on the understanding that it's impossible to love someone unconditionally if we can't love ourselves in the same way.

When we are constantly busy rejecting, judging ourselves, comparing ourselves with everyone around us, attacking and belittling ourselves, we inevitably do the same with the people around us, especially those closest to us. The most vital step then to be able to change our (failed or failing) relationships and base them on love, is to begin to love ourselves.

And that is the 'how'.

To begin to tell another person the truth about ourselves is a test of the strength of our undertaking to free ourselves from the superego's tyranny; it's like cutting the bridges behind us and coming out into the open, declaring frankly, 'Here I am with my judgments, my fears, my weaknesses, my envy, jealousy, possessiveness, and also with the courage to look at all these feelings.'

When we take this step we strike a heavy blow to the judge's tyranny: we no longer keep skeletons in the cupboard; there is no more pretending, there are no more masks that hide our shadows, or rather, those that the superego calls our shadows.

The more we can reveal our true selves to ourselves and to those we love, the more our unconscious will be within our reach and the easier it will be to contact those parts of us that we had to deny, repress and hide to make mum and dad happy.

The love that is freed in the relationship, its capacity to support our exploration and the courage that it requires, inflames the desire to be free, free to live in the present and to delight in our life and the richness of our being. Our husbands, our wives, our friends, our children can become the strongest allies and the most solid supports of our passion to be alive.

The 'how' is achieved by unmasking the superego and identifying those ways in which we reject ourselves and sabotage our growth. If we are not able to consciously defend ourselves from our judge's attacks, we won't be able to defend ourselves from attacks from others.

If we are not clear in our intention to honor our individuality and discover its uniqueness, it will be very difficult for us to respect and love others for their individuality, and we will continue to consider their behavior wrong and antagonistic. Worse still, we will find ourselves bogged down in an impossible attempt to change the people around us.

We can begin to build the foundations for a real change in our intimate relationships, by assuming the responsibility for changing our inner relations with our superego and basing the relationships on our desire for love and freedom instead of on fear, control and dependence.

Extend an invitation

This openness inevitably becomes an invitation to our partner. When this invitation is accepted, then the couple has a common ground of engagement, respect, honesty and intention. In such a relationship, both people (whether husband and wife, lovers, friends) begin to practice a conscious communication that involves an awareness of the superego's presence and activity.

For example, they can become aware of the way they project their own judge onto the other, punish each other, attack each other and create conflicts; the way they create guilt and shame, shy away from challenging the other's judge, express their hostility in a direct or indirect way and so on.

A common commitment can allow a couple to begin to trust each other; to support each other in the process of liberating themselves from their superego, and not be afraid of change.

A common commitment in this direction also leads the people involved to face and challenge the roles they identify with in the relationship: husband, wife, father, mother, son, authority figure, victim, brother, sister, good friend, sexual object, the helper, controller, and so on. This enables a person to become aware of the rigidity of their own identification and its intrinsic limitations.

Furthermore, this communion of intent towards love and freedom allows the couple to have a real intimacy without fear of being attacked. Then, it's possible to show and share their vulnerability.

Freedom from the past

The communion of intent becomes the basis for letting go of the fundamental fear of being wrong and all the associated anxiety.

With time, the fundamental differences between a relationship based on the superego and on transference and one where both partners are actively engaged in rebelling against the superego's tyranny, will become apparent.

The first – love based on the superego connection – chains. The second – love based on awareness and true intimacy – liberates. We can be free from the conditioning of our parents and the superego's presence in our present life. Free from the past.

> The unconscious controls the present by virtue of not being available to consciousness. It is not available to consciousness because of the ego defenses, which are necessary for the ego to defend itself, at least in part, against the superego. The resulting situation is the transference of the past onto the present, and the consequent loss of reality. From this perspective, we see that self-realization is equivalent to the end of transference. And because transference is maintained partly by the superego, freedom and self-realization mean in part the dethronement of the superego.
>
> (A. H. Almaas, *Work on the Superego*, Diamond Books, Berkeley CA, USA, 1992, p. 10)

Inquiry, meditations and visualizations

This inquiry relates to your feelings about and responses to a person with whom you have a current, intimate and important relationship. The first time you do this inquiry, the ideal is to do it alone. Begin by telling yourself the truth about the way you relate to the person/people you love.

Next time you do the inquiry, be brave enough to do it with the other person in this relationship. At that point you will face an essential passage for release from the superego: you begin to tell the other the truth about yourself, take off your mask and, courageously, face the fear of being judged, rejected, hurt and betrayed.

Observe very carefully the way your superego attacks you while doing this inquiry. Observe and note the physical reactions.

It can give you some essential keys to understand your inner dynamics with the judge in your relationships: very often we attack the other in the same ways our judge attacks us, and very often we defend ourselves from the other's attacks with the exact same unconscious reactions with which we try to avoid our superego.

1. Close your eyes and let yourself think, remember, feel a current intimate and important relationship. Observe which physical sensations manifest, which emotions surface. Note if there's an absence of emotions; if there are any immediate judgments with regard to the other person and to the dynamics of the relationship. Observe if there is resistance in doing this exercise and if defenses are activated. Continue to keep your attention on your body and feel what happens physically while you are connecting internally to that relationship and the way you live it.

2. What are your main judgments toward the other person in this relationship? Observe what happens to you when you formulate those judgments: what happens in your body, what emotions and thoughts come to the surface. Ask yourself what these prejudices have to do with you: are you projecting onto the other person something that belongs to you? Do you see your father or mother in him or her? What do you gain by keeping those judgments?

3. Explore the way you attack the other person with those judgments. Think about the situations in which you attack. How do you feel after the attack? What physical sensations

do you feel when you attack the other?

4. Explore the way you allow the other to attack you and the way you react to these attacks: do you counterattack, do you run away, do you freeze, do you pretend nothing has happened, do you deny yourself completely? Anything else? What is your preferred way of dealing with attacks? What do you feel in your body when you are under attack in relation to your defenses?

5. Explore how you react when your beloved withdraws their affection. Do you punish or avenge yourself on the beloved for withdrawing their love?

6. What are the main situations of conflict that arise with the other? What judgments do you hold? What would happen if you let those judgments go?

7. Imagine being completely honest in this relationship. Can you do it? What are the obstacles to total honesty? Is it possible for you to be vulnerable in this relationship? Is it possible for you to accept the vulnerability of the other? If not, what is it that frightens you?

Chapter 12

The Spiritual Meaning of the Inner Judge

The superego is, probably, our principal obstacle at the beginning of our journey towards consciousness and self-realization.

In previous chapters, we learned that at the heart of our relationship with the superego, there is fear of death and of disappearance; the fears experienced in childhood, and the consequent adaptation to family conditioning in order to avoid those fears and the pain associated with them.

We have seen how, on becoming adult, the superego's presence and the dynamics of our relationship with it condition our daily life and reduce our experiences to manageable and partially controllable events. We know how this dynamic keeps us in an essentially childish state where our sense of worth depends on the acceptance and recognition of the superego (internally) and of others (externally).

The past's shadow pervades

We may be able to recognize, now, how this continuous engagement of our attention to the inner dialogue/conflict between authority (superego) and child, shifts our consciousness to mere mental activity and, therefore, how any experience we have feels energetically depleted, repetitive, flat, without vitality or excitement.

The shadow of the past, with all its associations, superimposes itself on what is happening here and now.

At the same time, we have seen how the superego carries out an essential function with regard to survival and our ability to navigate this world; a world where every individual has to come to terms with different structures of social control, ethical and moral values, ethnic and national customs and habits, conventions, standards of behavior and so on.

The superego also offers us a sense of identity based on a particular image of ourselves that it constantly re-creates both inside and out, and defines our perception of space and the way we live in it.

Often a well-formed superego has this double face – the tyrant and the enlightened monarch – and, depending on which face it shows, uses different methods to assert its power. But it is always concerned with power.

Oppression and freedom

We have seen how it is not the content of judgments and prejudices that makes the presence of the superego restrictive; rather it is the methods it uses to maintain the status quo that keep us oppressed.

At the core of the superego is a repressive structure that has an aggressive energy, whether it is explicit and comes through as orders, reproaches and challenges, or is indirect and surfaces through manipulations, complaints and blackmail. The point is, we constantly find ourselves having to reckon with that aggression, an expression of its power.

Our potential for growth is limited, dramatically, by the fact that a large part of our vital energy is engaged in defending ourselves against possible attacks from the superego, and by the effort required to keep repressed materials in our unconscious.

Osho talks about going beyond the boundaries defined by conditioning, integrating ever greater portions of the unconscious until we accept it in all its manifestations; it is growth in all directions and dimensions that leads to a crystallization of the ego, and opens the doors to what Osho defines as 'individuality'.

Individuality is the manifestation of our true identity and the fulfillment of every one of us as a unique and unrepeatable manifestation of the Absolute. Individuality acknowledges that every one of us is a unique incarnation of the Divine, of the Universal Mind, of the noumenon.

It is impossible to transcend the ego while its growth is inhibited or conditioned by the superego's presence. In fact, in order that the ego can grow it needs to expand and to know itself in a myriad of dimensions that the superego blocks, judging them dangerous and unwieldy, dimensions that belong to living and not to simple survival.

Contact with Essence

At the core of Osho's teachings is the image of Zorba the Buddha – representative of Osho's understanding of the non-separation between matter and spirit and the necessity to develop, simultaneously, our humanity and divinity.

In his book, *The Psychology of the Esoteric*, Osho details the movement of growth involving the full spectrum of human potential and talks of the seven levels of consciousness and the human's seven bodies. The fifth of the bodies is the spiritual body or level of crystallized individuality.

The opportunity to come into contact with the existential dimensions of Being – Essence – requires that within us there exists an inner space where these dimensions can reveal themselves and be perceived. In general, our inner space is full of emotions, thoughts and feelings linked to the unconscious relationship between ego and superego and to the conflict between 'have to' and 'to be'.

And one of the most intense misunderstandings we face on our journey is the belief that the ego must be wiped out, destroyed, uprooted, in order for us to enter into our spirituality. This belief directs our attention in the wrong direction as well as giving us an impossible task.

By concretely experiencing being the personality – the body, the mind, the emotions – as well as the soul, the essence, we can know ourselves as being the totality and unity of all this, and of existing in all these dimensions simultaneously. When this knowing is completely integrated then we can stop trying to be different from what we are (which is what our superego wants) and we can start to discover the richness and uniqueness of the totality that we are, accepting and integrating all the forms of our being.

With this understanding, the superego is seen as both an obstacle on our path as well as, at the same time, an enormous opportunity. As metals are transformed by the fire of the blacksmith, our consciousness, our intelligence, our love and our commitment are forged in the daily challenge of finding an adult relationship with the superego, and the ability to be ourselves and to live our experience in a creative way and without prejudices.

We grow up acknowledging, becoming intimate with and integrating those authority figures that, by conditioning our growth, have contributed to the formation of the personality. But, finally, we recognize it as a false identity or, if you prefer, the outward suit, the appearance, the social mask that hides and protects our true nature. We acknowledge that we are constantly comparing our sense of value and our personal authority against the worth of every external authority.

Training ground

The conflict between ego and superego is, basically, our best training ground for learning how to overcome seeing conflict as destructive and repressive and for moving to a new and less primitive environment where conflict can be lived as creative tension, as a motor for evolution, and as a forge for the crystallization of the ego.

> ... the issues and the conflicts of the personality are not haphazard and meaningless; they are not simply barriers to realization and liberation. They are related in specific ways to

the states of realization themselves, to the states of being. To gain a more precise understanding of the situation, and to personalize the teaching, we need first to understand the personality and how it is related to the free reality, the being – what we call essence. Our true nature, our essence, what is real and unconditioned in the human being, does not exist in some mysterious realm, waiting for us to attack and slay the inimical ego, and then show up in glory. Our being, our essence, the divine within us, is connected to our personality in a very complex and intimate way.

(A. H. Almaas, *The Elixir of Enlightenment*, Samuel Weiser, York Beach, USA, 1998, p. 29)

Without doubt, the inevitable task for us, as we move towards openness to the dimensions of Being as they manifest in us and in the world around us, is to become aware of the presence of the superego, and take responsibility for our internal dynamic and the way it is projected externally in our relationships.

When we start being able to look at ourselves without judgment, comparison and prejudice, then we will accord that same behavior to the world around us; the resolution of the inner conflict will, inevitably, be reflected externally.

On the wall of the house of a friend of mine in Australia, a wise woman and healer, I found these lines on a piece of paper:

When I accept your quietness
And not assume it is because of me
When I accept your anger
And not react as if you are angry with me
When I can allow you to be indifferent
And not take it as an insult
When I can be with your company
And not see your behaviours as a reflection on me
When I can accept your swings of mood

Without needing to understand or control
When I can allow you to be you
I will be beyond ownership
Then, my dear friend, not only will you feel my love
But I will have truly found freedom within me.

Chapter 13

I Am

Imagine how it would be if one morning while you were still in bed and waking up, you suddenly realized that there was silence in your head. No chatter, no back-and-forth about what you had to do or not to do; no pressure to make plans or to be ready for something.

Imagine how it would feel in your body. Perhaps the feeling would be like lying down and being enveloped by a soft cloud of silence.

You might feel directly, and simply, aware of your body, without your usual concepts and judgments. You would be astonished at the simplicity of sensations without mental content, as if everything had... yes, more substance!

You might also notice that you feel your body as a complete unit, not in pieces; rather, something that exists as a whole.

As you focus your attention on that part of your body that is touching the mattress, you notice that you can feel pressure, heat, density, but you can't feel the boundary between mattress and body. How strange! It feels as if there is no separation between your skin and things around you!

You may ask yourself, 'But isn't the skin my house? Isn't the skin the boundary that defines who I am (what is inside) and that which is not me – what is outside my skin?' The thought, surfacing for a moment, slips away, leaving a void and silence. You hear drops falling on the balcony, music drifting from the next apartment and your breath going in and out, and you feel a light coolness on your upper lip. Everything is so clear.

Suddenly you understand that this clarity is due to the fact that everything is as though it were submerged, but also accentuated by the silence and the interval between one event and the next.

But something is missing, something is absent. Ah, of course! There are no judgments, evaluations or comments. Everything appears and disappears in its purity: a thought, a feeling, an image, a breath, an emotion. It's just as the great mystics have said, for centuries – everything appears like waves in the ocean of consciousness.

As you continue to enjoy this simple tranquillity you notice the absence of tension; you feel no need to grasp at anything, you don't want to define and box anything. And no effort is required and there is no need to make any effort. It's like being at the cinema, relaxing in a beautiful, comfortable armchair enjoying life flowing inside and outside and you cling to nothing.

And yet, it's not exactly like that. It is so much more. You are life that flows and unfolds; life is not inside you, life is you! Oh God, that's too much! You ask yourself, 'Am I life?' And the question echoes in the silence.

To be ourselves fully, spontaneously, and authentically, means simply to be. Not to be a reaction, not to be determined or influenced by image or experience from the past, not to be according to memory and mind – is to simply be ... In simple terms, to experience ourselves as Being is to experience our existence as such, to experience our own presence, our own 'suchness' directly. It is the simplest, most obvious, most taken-for-granted perception that we exist. But this existence is usually inferred, mediated through mind, as in Descartes's 'Cogito ergo sum' – 'I think therefore I am'. Existence is background, not foreground, for our ordinary experience. To penetrate into this background, to question our assumptions about reality and our selves, allows us to encounter directly the immense mystery of the arising of our consciousness and of the world.

(A. H. Almaas, *The Point of Existence*, Diamond Books, Berkeley CA, USA, 1996, p. 19)

When the judge is silent for the first time, it's such a wonder!

You are alone at last, without your father or your mother, without keepers, without chattering voices, advising and reproaching, without prejudices to uphold and defend, without opinions to fight for, without ideals to die for.

You are alone, and the absence of voices and judgments allows you – for the first time – to be yourself, home at last! Into the space, freed of the judge, emerges an incredible creativity, a continuous explosion of possibilities and an astonishing mystery.

You are not alone; you simply are.

Part 4

Experiences

How does all that you have been reading show in life, every day, when we struggle with survival, in our work, with our friends and clients, in relationships and within ourselves, when we might feel that it is all too much?

In this fourth part of the book the understanding and the practice of consciously defending from the attacks of the superego and transforming the inner dynamic take flesh and bones through questions and answers, in Chapter 14, and through the contributions of some friends and colleagues in Chapter 15.

In these flesh and bones you might find your own story, episodes of your life, your frustrations, your own questions and realizations, the glory and beauty of a more present consciousness.

They are all very personal when they address challenging moments and patterns in someone's life, as well as when they focus on specific therapeutic issues in great detail and with deep participation.

Chapter 14

Questions and Answers

Question – How can I identify the superego?
Sometimes I am confused about what the superego really is. A while ago, for example, a dear friend from the past came to see me. We spent quite a while together, but then I began to feel that I needed my space, and, at the same time, I felt a level of stress and insecurity about how to proceed. I could feel it as a sensation in my body along with a voice, on the one hand, saying that it's better to be alone and on the other that I am too alone. In that case, I sense there is a conflict between two parts, of which one is certainly the superego. But how can I distinguish them? As I got caught in my inner dynamic, I started cutting off from my friend and we left each other with a certain coldness.

Answer – Both your responses are evidence of the judge!
In both cases, there is a judgment: the first says, 'It's better to be alone', the second, 'You are too alone'. The two judgments are part of the same dynamic and represent the polarities of the conflict.

Let's take a step back to the moment you feel, after having spent some time with your friend, that you want to have some space away from her. In that moment your inner reality is your desire for space and if there is no judgment (one way or another) but a simple acceptance of the situation, then you may be free to act in a way that recognizes that need. In this case, you could simply communicate your need to your friend.

However, as you feel insecure about expressing what you need in the moment, what is more likely happening is that in order to support your wish for space you need to justify it internally with a judgment that generalizes the situation ('it's better to be alone' takes the place of 'I would like to be alone now' inside of you).

In that moment you shift from what you really feel to an abstract concept and you identify with your judge (particularly that aspect which has to do with commanding) that tells you the way reality is 'in general'. You are taken away from the present moment – the living situation – and your attention is redirected to an abstract 'it's better to be alone'. Alongside that, you identify with another attack from the judge (the one that makes you feel wrong) that tells you that you already stay alone too much. Both these attacks don't fit with what you know you are feeling and so you feel guilty and punish yourself for 'committing the sin of wanting to be alone' while you 'should' be with your friend.

Both judgments reject your simple need to have space and they shift your attention to the mental and emotional dynamics of what is right or wrong and how you should, or should not be. If at that point you defend yourself against the first attack, then you won't need to react by blaming yourself for wanting to be alone and punishing yourself by withdrawing your energy. This might have created a feeling of separation from your friend.

Afterwards (or together with your friend if they are available), you can explore what is happening and see whether there is a tendency in you to isolate yourself and to use the need of space as an excuse to withdraw, or not. Watch the way the whole dynamic arises from the simple rejection of that feeling of wanting some space for yourself.

Every time we reject the present, an attack is being carried out by the superego that tells us that the reality, and ourselves in it, should be different from the way it is. In this case, paradoxically, the attack arrives by denying the need of the moment – 'space now' – and introducing a generalization that takes you away from the moment and the current situation, plunging you into an internal dynamic which is almost depersonalized and mental.

*Q. How come I can identify one judgment and even counter it,
and then there is immediately one waiting behind it?*

**A. Zen Masters say that it is a dog's nature to bark and, in the
same way, it is a judge's nature to judge.**
It is impossible to stop the judge from judging. In fact, as I
outlined before, the judge is merely a mechanism, a program of
conditioning implanted in early age with the scope of facilitating
our survival through a specific set of rules and within a specific
context of values. The mechanism operates through a constant
evaluation of reality based on judgments – a repetitive,
continuous, oppressive flux of judgments – mostly flowing in a
subconscious way and ready to pop into the conscious mind.

To counteract the judge we need to remember to shift our
attention from the specific judgment to the mechanism. We need
to remember the myth of Medusa: cutting one snake at a time will
not work as another immediately grows to take its place.

In the same way, as you deal with one judgment and counter
it, another is already waiting. The point then, is to directly
counter the mechanism that produces the judgments and not the
particular example. There are a multitude of them. What you
need to do is to switch off your computer rather than merely
close all the programs but leave the processor running.

You are in charge! Cut the head off the Medusa! Be present
and see the judge attacking you and notice your habit of reacting
unconsciously and getting involved with the judgment.
Recognize the mechanism in action. Stay present and use your
will to avoid engaging and reacting. Stay present and use your
vitality and strength as your sword to stop the attack. Stay
present and recognize what you are experiencing in the moment
beyond judgment and evaluation. This conscious presence will
behead Medusa.

Q. I have difficulty getting in touch with my anger.
I have been able to do some work with this emotion and I see,
again and again in my childhood and adolescence, my angry
mother. All memories remind me of her in this way. It's re-
emerged also that at certain moments she threatened to kill
herself. Her energy was so strong that I was frightened of it; I felt
guilty for her dissatisfaction and the incomprehension that she
felt she was receiving. I was so frightened that up to a few years
ago, I would react with shock each time anyone around me was
angry or raised their voice.

I also observe that the idea of my parents' death flusters me; I
feel guilty, and uneasy, and that the superego is still active there
and attacks me, telling me that it's my fault if they do die, as I
don't love them enough.

Also, I am often in the role of the person that 'doesn't love
enough' in my relationships and don't allow myself to relax in
the love I feel. I keep busy negotiating with my partner, trying to
prove my interest, instead of defending myself from my inner
judge and silencing it.

I have, however, successfully managed to identify the judge's
more obvious attacks and am often able to neutralize them – so
much so that my life has tangibly improved; I feel freer, more
vital, more joyful.

At the same time I also have the capacity to pay more
attention to the indirect and manipulative methods that the
judge sometimes uses and that are not easy to recognize. They
often concern the sense of value I place on different aspects of
myself: as a woman, in business relations, in love affairs and in
regard to my creativity. I see the attack when it has already
arrived and I have suffered it; the energy is lost, and there is a
sense of defeat, impotence, frustration and I recognize that it is
still my mother.

The symptoms are clear, I am left high and dry, and I fall. It's
clear. My value is linked to the support.

A. The sense of self-worth is probably the fundamental aspect attacked by the superego.

The message you are receiving is, 'You have no intrinsic value. Your worth is defined by your relationship with me (the judge) and by your being acceptable and recognized by me (the judge).' Through the dynamic of control – based on judgments, prejudices, values and standards of behavior originally defined by parents – the judge denies you any intrinsic value. You are not simply worth something because you exist; you are only worthy if you behave in a certain way which is defined by the judge itself.

So, if you are as your mother wants, she loves you and everything is in order, but if you don't behave in an acceptable way (according to her criteria) then you hurt her and (according to your thinking, or sometimes her proclamation) you will probably be the cause of her death. This is a classic example of the Italian (but not only Italian) mother's cry: 'You'll be the death of me!' Generally the superego, in its role of the internalized mother, attacks you in a more indirect, non-frontal, way, bargaining with love – if you give me your will and if you are, and do, as I want, then I love you.

This is probably the most difficult form we have to deal with and defend ourselves from. It is more subtle and deceitful than the frontal attack. It makes us feel bad if we choose the freedom to be ourselves and make our own mistakes. It makes us feel wrong and ungrateful and pushes us to radically cut off any life force that contains rebellion.

Rather than hurt the mother inside us we prefer to turn our aggression against ourselves; aggression that, as we have seen, is only a distorted manifestation of our vitality. Moreover, as you have observed, worth is connected to support.

If you have not been supported, how can you have a sense of your worth? If only what comes from the superego is worthy, how can you support your own worth without coming into conflict with it (the judge)? And when you are yourself and act in ways that you think are right for you, then you don't behave as your superego (mother) wants and this is the proof that 'you don't love her enough'.

It is important to realize that, as long as even a small part of you is still convinced that there is some truth in all this, you will continue to create emotional situations where you find yourself in this dynamic and identify with the woman 'that doesn't love enough'.

A complete resolution of this issue in your life must include:

1. Understanding the mechanism and its origin (the relationship with your mother and the way in which your judge attacks you using the same original form)
2. Being able to consciously defend yourself against the judge's attacks (inside and outside), thereby freeing your vitality and reconnecting yourself to the sense of your intrinsic worth
3. The complete disidentification from the particular self-image that keeps on re-creating externally and internally a specific identity (the one that 'doesn't love enough')
4. Finally, the letting go of a specific image of your body linked to this internal dynamic. It is a process where you consciously decide to support yourself when confronting the inner judge and the fears that it generates in relation to your parents.

It is essential for moving away from guilt, from fear and the habitual spiral of reactivity, to learn how to give space to your rage in a conscious way using meditations, breathing techniques and focused exploration. Moreover, confronting your internal dynamics with the judge allows you, in the long run, to perceive your parents in a more direct and loving way, without those filters that stem from childhood experiences.

Q. I work continuously... I haven't time to stop, and when I can do it, on rare occasions, I can't be quiet... If I have nothing to do, I invent something to fill my time.

I feel as if I am a machine... full of responsibilities that most often succeed at hiding a restless mood. Amid all this chaotic movement, which I always try to control, I manage, at times, to enjoy myself. It's a way of filling my life that, otherwise, would be too empty; I can't seem to be able to put order in myself so I put order in others.

I am tired of telling myself that I would love to solve this dilemma, and I'm bored with the fact that I never solve it; I am bored with myself.

So, come what may, I fill my life with work. My reasoning? If I work, at least I earn and then, who knows? I am tired of chasing a dream, I have lost my innocence. I have stiffened my walls.

To say all this makes me sad. I have never shown my fragility until now. Everyone wants me to be Super. Now I understand why everybody calls me to tell me their problems but they never ask me my pains. It's because I don't share my pains! What's this nonsense!

I am speaking about things that I have rarely told anybody; well, only very few. The other things remain inside me and I don't have the courage to tell them even to myself and when they come to the surface I wall them up so I don't have to hear.

A. What is it you are trying to fill?

Why do you run from that 'something', as most people do, with such determination? What is the lack, the anxiety, the restlessness that grabs and terrifies you when the emptiness we all try not to feel begins to surface?

If, instead of escaping, we decide that the time has arrived to look and feel what's happening inside us, when all the substitutes and compensations cease to have meaning and satisfaction, then what we often discover is that feeling of emptiness together with a lack of clarity about what we are missing and an unpleasant sense of helplessness.

And so it is: something *is* missing, something so fundamental that in the long run nothing fills the space – not money, success, work, sex, alcohol, television, relationships; none of these can permanently fill that vacuum. None of these can give us a sense of deep satisfaction and completeness.

The superego does all it can to prevent us from looking into that emptiness: it pushes us 'not to waste our time with this foolishness' and convinces us that it is only a fantasy to try and know ourselves; that we need to 'come to terms with reality'. It fills us with 'good sense' by inviting us to forget our desperation, it manipulates us with the promise that 'one day it will be better', it deceives us with images of sacrifice and redemption that will come when we make our husband happy, our children, our wife, people we love. The voice says, 'Wait, wait a little longer, do it for them, you can't be living for yourself...' And so, day after day, we continue to fill that vacuum with all that we can, until it works for us (or so it seems).

The emptiness that frightens you so much is also a door through which you can find yourself. That vacuum is so terrifying because somewhere deep inside you, you know that most of what you live is a pretence, a habit, a contract. You know that it is true that you are missing something deeply, and that something is you.

That connection with your being was broken and forgotten many years ago, so many, that you have even lost the awareness of what you have lost: your worth, your vitality, your peace, the joy of simply being yourself.

But at the same time that vacuum continues to be felt, that inner voice that knocks at your heart, that dream that pushes to become reality. The Being knocks continuously at our door; its potential wants to be actualized and the repression imposed by the judge becomes more and more disempowering and absurd.

That's why so many people arrive at old age full of resentment and bitterness: an entire life passed by denying themselves.

And for what? Survival? Survival of what? Of a control mechanism that we took on when we were children and had no other choice, and were not capable of taking care of ourselves.

Growing up means becoming the master of your home and stopping being the unconscious slave, the disheartened victim of a past that makes no sense other than what you give it (by creating it again and again).

This 'thing' that you miss is the most precious thing that a human being can find: the direct experience of yourself, of your existence, of your worth. It is a direct perception of your individuality and uniqueness beyond the recognition and acceptance of others. It's that divine spark that exists without the need to be in a certain way, or to be as others want you to be. It waits patiently for your attention and acknowledgment.

Q. The more aware I am of the superego's processes, the more I realize that it attacks me about deeper and deeper levels of my issues and related defenses.
What this is like is almost an escalation but in reverse order, towards the core. Sometimes the judge appears to me as a master. Even so, it's often hard and I feel worn out! Can you tell me about this process and the way I can 'take a break' without returning mechanically to the unconscious defenses or compensations?

A. This is evidence of growth! The superego's attacks become more violent as the awareness of our inner dynamics with it grows.
How does this happen? In a sense, the judge begins to use the new understandings and intuitions that you have been experiencing, as ammunition, as something to hold against you. But mostly what is happening is that your physical, emotional and mental sensibility is greater.

The process of inner growth is, fundamentally, a process of expanding consciousness, and release from layers and layers of insensibility (the defenses that have allowed us to survive, maintaining in the unconscious the pain of the separation from our Being). This also means that we continuously feel the judge's attacks with greater intensity and precision.

It is necessary to go through this phase. It is a kind of healing-crisis in which we build our capacity to consciously defend ourselves from the judge while keeping our focus on the reality of our experience without judgment or evaluation.

Usually the superego's attacks have to do with the more superficial layers of our personality and self-image because we live a more superficial life, but the more we enter our unconscious and free the repressed material, the more the attacks will relate to essential elements of our story and identity.

These attacks, as you have noticed, are directed more and more towards core elements of your structure. We say that, more and more, the superego attacks where the deepest wounds are; but in so doing it shows, without wanting to, the key themes of the identification with your personality and those images of yourself that you are more attached to.

Obviously this process is painful, but also extremely revealing. Your ability to consciously defend yourself from the judge's attacks (that you created over time) allows you now to observe and listen to the content of the attack and be aware whether there's anything that can help you to be yourself.

The judge doesn't always say foolish things, and it's not always wrong. As most parents are, it also is motivated by the desire to protect you and teach you to survive, and often it is able to point us in the right direction. The problem, as we have seen, is not the content but the form it takes – one of aggression or manipulation.

When you are able, thanks to the work you have done, to defend yourself and not compulsively react to the aggression or manipulation, there is a space to observe the content and eventually, to use it in your favor.

Consciously defending yourself also brings to the surface the fatigue that comes with unconscious defense. A huge part of our energy is usually busy mechanically defending ourselves from the attacks. When we become conscious, this laborious wall becomes conscious too. For a while it continues as it always did, until conscious defense becomes so natural and fast that only a very small part of our vital energy is engaged. This energy is fundamentally one of survival, and can be used by our consciousness in turn, becoming creativity, clarity, passion, curiosity.

The best way to avoid returning habitually to defending and compensating is to defend yourself with even more determination in a conscious way and with absolute care not to get involved with the judge. This absurd cycle of attacks and reactions, happening in a subconscious way, is what sucks your energy.

That means to act immediately as the symptoms arise, without waiting or postponing: as soon as you feel guilt you know you are under attack!

As soon as you become tense and feel shame you know you are under attack!

As soon as you feel belittled you know you are under attack, and so you immediately defend yourself, without wasting a second.

Q. I spent all night tossing and turning. I was incapable of relaxing.

I had a constant sensation of nervous tension in my body; I woke exhausted. I stayed in bed to make inquiry on how I was feeling and I realized that the judge was making me feel guilty and pushing me to do, do, do something instead of being still in bed.

Up to this point there was nothing new, but as I stayed in bed, with awareness, I suddenly found myself in my mother's womb and there wasn't any difference between her superego (that drove her to always be doing something) and me. Even more upsetting, it felt like a physical pressure, constriction and agitation in my body – my superego that was directly connected with my mother's superego and with all feminine lineage from which I descend.

I knew my grandmother, and I remember well that feeling that we always needed to be 'doing' something. After this episode, I feel sure that was also the case with her mother and the mother of her mother, and so on. I'm not able to countercheck, but the sensation is very clear – a kind of genealogical tree of the superego!

Anyway, beyond the hypothesis, I found this experience very important: the judge with its genetic lineage stored in the body. In my case: grandmother, mother, me!

A. This is understandable and confirms that the superego's presence is cellular.
It is not sufficient to understand the superego and to face it psychologically; it's also necessary to single out the physical symptoms that are related to the judge's function.

While Freud traced the formation of the superego to the oedipal phase of childhood growth, C. G. Jung included the question of heredity through the presence of universal archetypes in the unconscious, with the introduction of the concept of the collective unconscious.

Jung indeed maintains that the psyche is an element within the evolutionary process; that the individual is connected to the past of all species, and their evolution, in that we all inherit a collective unconscious.

The process occurs because psychological archetypes – original characters that define a fundamental part of our personality – exist as energetic quantities in the collective unconscious and influence our behavior, our values, the way we see ourselves and others, the choices we make, the way we see the world and so on.

With the thinking of Wilhelm Reich entering the world of psychology, a new territory of understanding opened which insisted that these psychological/emotional mechanisms and representations exist with great force on a physical level – like a web of physical tensions and energetic contractions.

This concept is of a cellular memory. No change on a psychological and emotional level is possible or permanent, if the neural passages that develop during the preverbal period of childhood are not reprogrammed.

This can be achieved through meditation; indeed, meditation indirectly reckons with our concepts, ideas and convictions, simply by creating an inner space where our essential nature can show itself without filters. This then activates the process of revitalization and healing.

Q. When I want to ask for help or something I need, I go into shock and panic. What can I do to support myself?

A. The question of support is crucial in the work with the superego and changes our relation with it.
Originally, the superego had the purpose of providing us with a structure of values and criteria of behaviors that would help us to survive. Our parents provided us with all the means they considered necessary for us to be an acceptable, responsible, successful person, who could manage 'in the right way' the requests and difficulties of social life.

The superego is, indeed, the know-it-all on our shoulder, incessantly commenting on our performance and comparing it with that of others.

Part of your conditioning is that you must be a strong person who can do things on your own; that it is dangerous to ask for help. This may be the fear of putting yourself in a position of emotional vulnerability and dependence, and/or of running the risk of being rejected.

You make a decision then, to do things on your own, to become set in your ways, stick out your chin, close the heart by refusing that unacceptable sensation of weakness and withdraw into your pride, declaring, 'Me, do I need someone or something? In your dreams!'

The anxiety generated by the waiting for the superego's attack is denied and removed, and with it the fear that provokes the possibility to be seen as vulnerable and, consequently, rejected.

This dynamic comes from a precise idea of yourself that was created in childhood; you needed to deny that part of yourself that has needs, in order not to lose your parents' love (or the love of one in particular) and to keep their support. Support that was given if you behaved in a certain way. In this case, that 'way' had to be neither weak nor needy.

Now, to support yourself in the present, means you can choose to:

- acknowledge this dynamic and its origins with greater precision
- acknowledge that panic and shock are not caused by asking for help and expressing your needs (actions that have not yet happened) but by waiting for the superego's attack if you carry out that action
- acknowledge what judgment it is you expect (the way you should or shouldn't be according to your judge)
- tolerate the presence of anxiety and of related emotions and defend yourself from the superego's attack by activating your aggression in defense of your right to have needs and ask for help
- accept your vulnerability and understand that this idea of yourself as a strong person limits your experience of self

- disidentify from the old self-image by taking responsibility and giving support to yourself in all your manifestations, including those rejected by the superego.

As we learn to recognize the presence of the inner judge in our life, we will change the way we relate to it and grow up beyond the relationship with our parents. We will learn to discriminate and choose what is useful to us and what is outdated and not necessary any more.

As we become free of our childish representations of our parents we will be able, for the first time, to really see and appreciate them in their humanness. A sense of natural self-confidence and clarity will arise, simple and direct. We will come to know who we truly are and to know our value. We will come to know and understand why existence wants each one of us, right here, right now.

Chapter 15

Contributions

Caroline Beumer-Peeters

Working in a private practice with mainly teens and adolescents asks for a somewhat different approach. Not in the least because most of them are not coming entirely voluntarily. Usually they are either sent by their parents, teachers, school psychologist, or they come as part of a rehabilitation program through a probation officer. Many of them have dropped out of school, had issues with the law, or are using drugs. Not exactly the cream of the crop, many would say. But what meets the eye is not necessarily what is really there.

Before there is any possibility of working together on anything, a platform for intrinsic motivation and cooperation has to be established. The question is how to accomplish that, when all of society (home, school, law) in their eyes has already failed them. In general they are, in spite of their young age, already so damaged and disappointed, that they are highly mistrusting of any authority figure. And many of them carry some kind of psychopathological disorder, such as ADD, ADHD, ASS, PDD-nos or borderline, diagnosed by the many authority figures they have already been presented to. Most of them enter the practice room with their eyes completely shut down on the outside world. With a dark look, heavy energy and many times even a hostile attitude. Expecting nothing but the worst. And who can blame them?

I remember vividly the first time a young man like that walked into my practice room. One look at him and I could feel my whole inside cramp, and fear came up, contracting the space in my chest next to my armpits. A big rubber ball sank into my stomach area, and immediately doubt set in. I felt myself small, frightened and incompetent. Of course the conversation didn't go too well at all. It left me puzzled about what had happened there. Speaking with colleagues, I heard they knew this feeling all to well. It was the reason why they preferred not to work with this age group.

Sitting down with this, I couldn't feel any gratification in such a decision. I remembered very clearly how awfully lonely my own adolescence had been, and how I craved for somebody to notice and help me through it. So I decided to look at my own responses instead, and work with them. Inquiry, although I had no idea what that was at that time, was the answer. Curiously inquiring into, and allowing myself to be in the experience, instead of wanting to fix or avoid the awkward feelings on the spot, I went into the same situation over and over again. Seeing more and more teens and adolescents every week. By allowing the feelings to be there, to observe them, I gave myself the opportunity to see what it had to say to me. And my, did it talk! In fact it never stopped talking to me, and it became my ally in working with this at first glance challenging age group.

Over the years they became the main part of my clientele, and I have never had any regrets. In fact, it was the best thing that could ever have happened to me in my professional life. Since I discovered how wonderfully honest and beautiful they are. How unwilling to compromise to their inner truth and their beliefs they are. They are perfect mirrors, which helps me to be truthful, transparent and not compromising too. With every session I learn and heal as much as they do, if not more.

Being at an age when their ego is starting to take on a more permanent shape, and peer and parental pressure makes them sometimes rigid and stubborn in their ideas, their true essence is still very close at hand, and visible like a diamond in the rough. Helping them to see it, get access to it and invite it to come out, is to me the most gratifying job there is.

As already said, first some work has to be done to establish a platform for cooperation. It is at this stage that some therapists tend to become stranded in their communication. Usually because they approach the client and his or her issue from their own perspective, easily finding themselves getting entangled within their own projections or goals. With teens and adolescents, from there it quickly all becomes nothing more than pushing against a closed door. While in fact it is quite easy to just walk around a bit and see if there's somewhere a window slightly opened.

To be able to do that requires a letting go of all your own set ideas, expert knowledge, personal and professional judgments and hidden goals. It requires the therapist to fully embrace the world-view of the adolescent, and work with an open mind and heart from an equal level. Which in truth is very easy, since it's a relief to be able to let go of so much heavy luggage. Carrying nothing, being in the not-knowing, maybe in the beginning feels somewhat uncomfortable. But gradually this space becomes more and more friendly, as trust kicks in that somewhere along the line, somehow, the answers will unfold between you and the other.

For this to be able to happen, a few things are required on the side of the young clients. Whatever it is they will be working on with you, they have to really own it. It has to be their goal, their dream, and their own chosen path. And to be able to embrace it as their own, they have to be able to see the advantages, the benefits. The answer to 'What's in it for me?' is really important to them. How else can they motivate themselves to do anything? There have to be gains, or if these are not immediately visible, at least the loss of disadvantages, of burdens or problems. Feeling ownership, and seeing its value, is crucial. But they also have to have trust, some kind of confidence, that they are able to achieve it. In the beginning that trust or self-confidence usually is low or even fully absent. It has to be slowly built, reconstructed by small achievable steps forward, steps that still have to be taken, as well as steps that are already made but were left unnoticed or seen as insignificant. The rough diamond is covered with a thin layer of soot, making it invisible to the eye. Luckily soot is easily removable by a gentle rub with a soft cloth. So choosing their own goal, seeing its value, having the confidence they can achieve it, and consciously experiencing progress, are vital parts of a successful journey. And last but not least it is also exceptionally important to constructively prepare and deal with setbacks, since setbacks are a normal part of learning, of everyday life. I've found that these five factors are essential when it comes to intrinsic motivation for teens and adolescents to get their lives on track, and to walk their own chosen paths and flower.

Jesse (20) is a very gifted young man. He is highly intelligent and creative. He has a natural talent for leadership and is usually well behaved. He was adopted at age three, after being left right after birth in an orphanage in Haïti. During his first years there he suffered from severe hunger and lack of adult attention. When he finally was adopted he was super friendly, always laughing and very playful. His adoptive parents loved him dearly and, for the first 11 years of his life, everything seemed to turn for the better. Getting good grades at school, having lots of friends, and a stable home, made him an ideal child. Problems started to arise when he turned 12 and went to high school. He didn't work, let his grades slip, played hooky with some shady friends, and started using soft drugs.

Now 20, he still hasn't managed to overcome his drug habit and suffers from periods of mild psychosis. Making commitments and keeping them is hard for him. Especially when these commitments are for his benefit. It seems he always finds unconscious ways to sabotage his own life. For four months he has been coming to my practice. His social worker wants him to get clean, finish some kind of school education and get a job. This is how our first meeting went:

Jesse enters the room with a baseball cap pulled deep over his eyes, so I cannot see them. He does shake the hand I offer, and then falls down on a chair, sitting mainly on his back, with his legs opened widely. I have to hide a smile over this typical monkey behavior. He shows he has balls, literally in this case.

We sit for a few seconds silently, opposite each other. He starts to get nervous and snaps at me in an unfriendly voice: 'Is this going to take long?'

I look at him and ask: 'What else do you have to do? We can make sure you can make it there on time if needed. No problem.'

J.: *'Hm, well, let's get on with it then.'*

Me: 'Great. I like it when people want to get to work and make the best of the time we have. What other characteristics do you have that make you eager to start?'

Jesse is somewhat surprised and looks at me from underneath his cap.

J.: *'Well, I just don't think this is going to work.'*

Me: 'So you are critical. That is indeed a great characteristic. It helps you to make wise choices. Can you think of even more?'

J.: *(Now taking off his cap and looking me straight in the eyes while sitting upright) 'What is this? Are you pulling my leg?'*

Me: 'By no means. Why would I?'

J.: *'Nobody asks questions like that.'*

Me: 'What do you mean by "questions like that"?'

J.: *'Questions about what I'm good at. Nobody has ever been asking me that. Everybody only wants to talk about my problems. Telling me what I shouldn't do.'*

Me: 'What would you rather talk about?'

There is a long silence. Jesse sits back in the chair, turning his baseball cap in his hands. Then when the silence begins to feel a bit awkward he starts to speak slowly.

J.: *'I do like to talk if people are really interested. I do talk. Mainly with my friends and my mom.'*

Me: 'Wonderful! What do you talk about with your friends or your mom?'

J.: 'Anything. With my mom I can talk about anything. Even about my experiences with drugs. And with my friends... it depends on with which ones. With some I talk about music, and with others I talk... well, about stuff. You know. The world as it is.'

Me: 'Wow! That's a broad variety of topics. Does that mean you have wide interests?'

J.: 'Yes, I believe I do.'

Me: 'What would you say if we took time to get into these things you are interested in while we meet?'

J.: 'It would certainly make it more worthwhile. That's for sure. But didn't I get this referral to you to get clean?'

Me: 'How do you feel about that?'

(Big silence followed by a big sigh)

J.: 'I would like to get rid of the habit. It's just that I've tried so many times. And I don't think I can do it. It always fails. I always fail.'

Me: 'Jesse, how would you like to spend the time we have in these meetings exploring if what you just said is really true or not?'

J.: 'Do you doubt it to be true then? Do you think I can do it?' (Long pause...) 'Of course you're going to say yes now. That's what you're supposed to say, I guess.'

Me: 'What would need to happen for you to be able to quit using drugs and stay clean? How would that be?'

J.: (Silence...) 'I would have to lose this feeling of worthlessness inside.'

Me: 'Wow. I am impressed that you know why you're using drugs. Not many people can tell so clearly, you know. What makes you so clear about it?'

J.: 'I've thought about it a lot. Also I talk with my mom about it.'

Me: 'What else makes you see so clear?'

J.: 'I've always been like that. As a kid I would drive my mom crazy sometimes with all my questioning. I'm always hungry for answers, so I think a lot. That's just who I am.'

Me: 'That's really great, Jesse. That is your ticket out of all this

– your genuine curiosity, no matter what. That is really fantastic. Now tell me more about this feeling of worthlessness inside.'

J.: *(Silence... After some time he starts crying.)*

Me: 'Just take your time. We're not in a hurry. There is plenty of time to explore this. Just tell me what you sense in your body right now.'

J.: *'It's a big, gigantic deep hole of emptiness, like a black hole in space. It sucks all the life out of me. It makes me shrink and vanish.'*

Me. 'Jesse, would you like to know more about what it is, and how you can make it stop sucking the life out of you?'

J.: *'More than anything in the world.'*

Me: 'Even when it will at some points be scary, and you still have to come here and not quit working on it?'

J.: *'Yes, I want to. I will come.'*

Me: 'What makes you want this, while you already have walked out on several other therapies? I want to know why you think this time you will do it.'

J.: *'Nobody else has talked about these things before. This is what I really want to talk about. Now it's getting interesting.'*

Me: 'Even when it will be hard work?'

J.: *'Yes. I'm sure.'*

Me: 'How can we prepare for those moments when it will be hard or even scary? What can you do to still keep on track in such moments? Think of support from friends or family, any strategies that might help you – whatever you can think of. Then when you come here next time, that will be the first thing we will talk about.'

J.: *'Why?'*

Me: 'Jesse, in every process there will be hard times. You probably have already discovered that over and over. It doesn't mean you have failed. It's just normal when you are learning things, exploring new territory, that there will be bumps in the road. In my opinion it's best to prepare for those bumps, so they won't make you fall. What do you think? Does this make any sense?'

J.: 'Yeah, I guess.' (Sigh...) Shit happens. That's a fact.'

Me: 'Yes, that is a fact. And preparing for it means we can keep our shoes clean.'

J.: 'Haha, that's a good one. I like that one. Clean shoes. Maybe that should be my tag. "Walk with clean shoes."'

Me: 'Yes, we are now both embarking on a new journey. "Project Clean Shoes". See you next time, Jesse. I'm looking forward to it.'

Jesse is now four months on the road with his 'clean shoes'. He still has a long way to go. So far he hasn't missed an appointment, and has managed to stay clean for several periods of time varying from 1 week to 12 days. On the days he is still using, he uses less than half of what he used before the therapy started, and he hasn't had any psychotic episodes since. He starts working in a printing shop next week for two afternoons. It's a promising start.

The story of Jesse's first appointment shows to me clearly how little one can prepare for a meeting like that. If I would have, would I have been able to see what was presented in that moment? Would I have been able to see the many gems that popped up in the conversation? They are already there, always, even if they come disguised as resistance in the beginning. To meet with an open mind and an open heart... It takes some courage to be in that space of not-knowing, unable to hide behind my expert status, I admit to that. It can feel shaky at times. But with what rewards? To meet a young man, seeing him opening up and sharing such beauty, such clarity, and intelligence. It leaves me in awe and deeply grateful again and again.

Caroline works as a solution-focused coach, counselor, therapist, trainer and author of several books on practical approaches to finding solutions with children and adolescents, and is currently CEO of a training institute. She works for international clients in a business environment, as well as in the field of children's and adult education with children, adolescents and adults. She has specialized in human behavior and trauma work. She is trained in fine arts, children's education, social psychology, sf-coaching and brief therapy, counseling, psychotherapy, hypnotherapy, color light therapy and SE-5 subtle energy alternative medicine.

Karuna Cinelli

I felt the need for freedom very early on; it has stayed with me for many years. When I was an adolescent it was expressed through rebellion against my mother and her control. In particular, it was freedom from her that I wanted. I imagined life far away from her suffocating presence as a paradise of enjoyment and happiness.

As I grew up, despite the physical distance from her, I continued to carry my past with me, or rather, my interpretation of an experience that continued to exist, not just as a memory, but as something which affected my emotions and feelings, affecting me on an energetic plane, the way I related to others and communicated, touching every aspect of my life. Inside I was still carrying my mum and dad, their values, their beliefs, their sense of duty, their behavior, their habits, without even realizing it. On the contrary, I thought I had unhooked myself from them by taking a different, to some extent, opposite route. Later I realized that my self-expression had been blocked; I didn't really know myself. Freedom was still far away, despite appearing to be free from my mother, from her direct control, and from my father.

It is through carrying out work on my inner judge that a great transformation has occurred in my daily personal and professional life. Understanding that the childhood conditioning received from one's family background creates a fundamental separation from oneself, from repressed parts which are removed from consciousness, remaining stifled and unconscious, has given me the means to examine myself. Giving value to my feelings, whatever they are, in order to perceive myself from a perspective of truth instead of a perspective of judgment, from negation and limitation, has accelerated a profound change that was already in motion.

The perspective of truth has been a decisive step towards myself, and it is for whoever wants to undertake and pursue a journey back from conditioning to freedom.

In the courses that the Integral Being Institute offers, one of the fundamental pillars in the work method used is acceptance. Acceptance is an openness and a way out from the judge's control, control that operates through judgments of unacceptability, with the focus of regulating the unconscious, sentiments, emotions and desires.

When I began to practice inquiry and open up I realized that the expression of my femininity had been penalized as my judge, my father, had considered it to be a weakness. On the other hand, my mother had provided me with feminine models that corresponded to deprivation, scarcity and sacrifice, which was another reason I assumed behavior that went against them.

On discovering this I realized that my life was a continual battle to demonstrate how strong I was, on top of the situation, and I suffered all the pain that this caused me, that was there somewhere alongside the frustration of having distanced myself from a quality that was so precious to me, that of being a woman. It is true that opening up is painful. It is a warning that the judge often uses to control access to the unconscious. Usually, the first phases are the most painful.

To the same extent, it is also true that the expansion of awareness brings with it resources that provide support during the discovery, such as compassion, love and trust.

What I experience and continue to see happening to many people is that their perspective of the truth gradually closes the distance between what we believe ourselves to be and who we really are, to the point of giving us the joy and relaxation of directly experiencing ourselves as we really are. This, for me, is freedom.

Conditioning isn't something that is static, that only belongs to the past; it continues to repeat and update itself over the course of time. All figures of authority that we come across, including spiritual masters, are readjusted and incorporated in our lives, creating a restricted behavioral track founded on 'having to be' and dependency.

The judge does all that it can to guarantee our survival, to make us feel secure. It gives us parameters of what is acceptable more or less ready-made according to the situation, the person concerned, in order to obtain approval, love, a sense of belonging to the family, society, the community.

As long as our reference is the inner judge, with its comments, judgments, evaluations, we also see it externally, projected on our friends, family, work colleagues, teachers and whoever is a figure of authority.

Our self-value will be in the hands of someone else, not only to the detriment of our true and free expression, which is a high price to pay, but to the detriment of the fundamental experience 'I am valuable'.

Self-recognition that 'I am valuable' brings an end to the internal conflict sustained by the judge and reconnects us to our Being, the spontaneous way our intrinsic intelligence deals with circumstances and works in the best possible way.

I note that I am becoming more open to trust, which has brought a new significance: I am able to live and support myself, drawing on resources that present themselves at the precise moment that I need them.

This is a gradual process that requires presence, perseverance in consciously defending oneself against the judge, and the courage to take responsibility for one's own life time after time.

Responsibility is a fundamental point where many people remain stuck for a long time. They are aware of the various mechanisms, of the automatic defenses, of the compensations, of their personal story and of their influence on the present, recognizing the attacks of the judge and its symptoms, but nevertheless no real change occurs.

Why is this? The habit of living in a vicious circle controlled by the judge is deeply rooted in each one of us; it is the territory that most people know and live in, despite the limits, the suffering, the lack of pleasure and loss of value.

Our attachment to the identification with our personal story, with the self-images built over time, is an obstacle with which we have to deal.

The child, insofar as it is the center of attention, insofar as it needs care and affection, is totally dependent on its parents. Getting OUT of this dependency turns us into adults and makes us responsible for ourselves.

This responsibility requires a fundamental shift from outside to in: from the judge to one's own energy, with the steady determination to keep it alive in such a way as to feel ALIVE. Where to be alive is radically different than surviving.

Survival is made up of strategies for not feeling; it is monotone, it cuts us out of the immediate experience of reality, it castrates us of our vital energy. At the same time, if we look at it from a child's perspective, it holds a series of advantages in terms of:

1. Keeping mum and/or dad happy
2. Not taking risks
3. Having a set identity
4. Being able to play the victim
5. Obtaining external recognition.

None of us are immune to this. The child that we were is here – it doesn't matter how old we are today; the automatic reaction to whatever the situation is is quick and precise.

Practicing ongoing conscious defense against the judge is a

must; it's not enough just to be conscious of it on a mental level. Putting it into practice means ongoing training, being alert and blocking the judge's maneuvers when it attempts to take control of our will.

Practice means aligning, it means identifying and carrying out our plans, it means going through daily life with integrity, love and passion. It requires direct involvement, the breaking of habits, of what is easy or taken for granted. For this reason it is not easy; for this reason sometimes we hinder ourselves and choose survival rather than taking risks and feeling the thrill of being alive.

Support in our conscious defense against the judge cannot come purely through applying a technique learned from reading a book or participating in a course. It is from the center of our being that we find the strength to be ourselves; the technique is but a means. The roar that shatters our conditioning originates from the wholeness of our core, not from the technique itself. Recognizing the inner judge, from where it comes and its implications on the present, removes one of the greatest obstacles in self-realization.

It opens the way for contact with our center, and from here, a complete answer occurs, present, healthy in that nothing is taken for granted; whatever it is, it recognizes and realizes who we really are.

From this perspective also the technique takes up a new place and significance in that it becomes a means for entering our center.

All centering techniques, rooting, meditation that involves the body, are not only just physical postures; they pull our energy towards the inside, immediately changing our focus from outside to in, from there to here.

It is the intention to be ourselves that we develop and this intention provides us with support and the direction towards our center.

By nurturing our center, the judge who waits in the doorway loses its power, becoming ever meeker; it loses its aggression, and also our relationship with it and with what it represents is transformed.

Our center is our true resource.

Karuna is a teacher and tutor at the Integral Being Institute.

Vinko Sandalj

I consider the seminar I participated in with Avikal on the inner judge to be one of the most useful pieces of work from a practical point of view in my daily life. The mechanism through which the judge manifests itself is very simple and easy to recognize: its thermometer is anxiety. It is a sensation of unpleasant insecurity, with one's heart in one's throat, often accompanied by slight tachycardia, like being hunted and not knowing where to run. That's the one, the judge on the attack! Recognizing it is, in the majority of cases, child's play.

By now it is very clear to me that anxiety is ALWAYS the work of the superego. When the feeling emerges I stop a moment and ask myself: who is unhappy with me at this moment, who says I'm doing something wrong and that I'm not on top of the situation? I would say that, in my case, it is always a paternal figure that reveals itself, but a figure that is slightly adapted to my needs. It could be my father as he really was, with a particular phrase or act, but often it's an actor, dressed to look like my father, who offers unexpected judgments on a new situation that was never real for him, but is very real for me at that particular moment. It is me myself who provides the details and the scenography before inviting him to play his part.

I remember the anxiety I had, for a great part of my life, a frequent companion which would return to accompany me for days on end, without me knowing why. It was often related to my relationship with the outside world, in particular with situations where I was put to the test, for example my presence in public, both in private and work situations. I felt timid, inadequate and severely criticized by others because of my lack of sociability and liveliness. A word or gesture that I believed to be wrong would haunt me for days on end, during which I just wanted to collapse. After having done the workshop about the judge, it became easier in these cases to individualize the role of my father; he was very real like he was in his life. Having a natural inclination to socialize, he made me feel inferior and I was thought to be more similar to my mother – timid and introverted, to be precise. In the same instant that I was able to recognize this mechanism, the anxiousness would disappear, immediately, effortlessly.

For some years I exercised and applied this technique and developed the ability to use it in the space of a few seconds. In this way I reduced, not only the time during which my anxiety revealed itself, but I also gradually diminished the number of times in which it appeared. In a work context a tool that provides such instant help is extremely useful. When anxiety still emerges, a fraction of a second is enough to see my father-judge behind the stage curtain and I immediately relax. A hundred courses specifically aimed at professional subjects could not have given me the security that I feel now in meetings and other situations.

There are still, however, periods in which, even if they are very rare, I am filled with anxiety for which I can give no explanation. They are situations that seem to be out of my control and in the hands of my invisible 'partner', the judge-father. In this case I wander in darkness and can't find the solution to the problem. It happened recently to me, on an occasion of grave financial crisis that involved an entire country and which had inevitable repercussions on my company. I had the same symptoms of anxiousness that I had had many years ago, profound and long-lasting, and I ruled out the possibility there could be a subliminal message from my inner judge, or at least one I could recognize. It seemed to me to be a classic, general situation, beyond any possibility of control, in which my poor dad couldn't have had any responsibility.

On my own I couldn't get out of it and I decided to speak with my therapist. With his help I began to follow a course that was parallel to what I had already followed on my own and I came across something familiar. Instead of analyzing the general situation that was obviously not in my power to change, we analyzed the significance it had for me and my company, in a family context. My company was the tool that my father had entrusted me with in order to support the family, and my job was to safeguard its operation and profitability. Any divergence would have involved a departure from the obligations I had taken on and would have meant betraying his trust, independent of any external causes. As soon as I understood this mechanism, my anxiousness dissolved and my general situation improved and, despite continuing to be serious, it didn't cause me anxiety anymore, leaving me free to take all the necessary decisions calmly and peacefully.

Since learning to manage this powerful technique of personal self-defense, I have become more self-confident and calmer in the presence of other people. I don't know which profound button this approach touches, but it is without doubt an extremely useful, everyday tool. What I refer to as anxiety could also be a sense of guilt for another person, but the understanding is the same. I use the technique of the inner judge to control my anxiety, but I think it can be used for other symptoms that function with a similar mechanism. Perhaps this research will be the subject of my next retreat with the inner judge.

Vinko is CEO of Sandalj Trading Company and a spiritual seeker.

Helen Anderson

Over many years I'd formed an identity as a corporate professional. It provided a base for me to feel a sense of belonging, and an identity as a successful, productive woman in the world. So why, about three years ago, did I find myself feeling disconnected, unfulfilled and bored? I had come to a crossroads where continuing as I was had little appeal, aliveness and purpose.

About this time I met Avikal, and the title of his book, *Freedom to Be Yourself*, completely resonated for me. Intuitively I felt my disconnection was with myself, and I wondered what it would take for me to feel differently; to feel the freedom of showing up as I am – without trying, and the effort of projecting and portraying a character I guessed other people, or society, or the corporate environment would find acceptable. At some level I was aware of my mask, and since this time I have been on the most intricate adventure, discovering more and more elements of my mask. They are sometimes amusing, sometimes devastatingly confronting; often I am in awe of the innate intelligence that decided to form the mask in a certain way to support me at certain times. Increasingly I have come to care for and respect elements of my mask that in previous times I was furiously keeping myself busy to avoid contacting. And it is so freeing, as there is less defensiveness and less protection and that frees more energy to live life.

In my work as an organizational development professional and executive coach, I have had a unique opportunity to work with many people across many different professions, industries and cultures. The universality of 'the mask' is striking, and the presence of the superego of course a constant. A number of the fundamental understandings I have learned from my work with the superego have been invaluable because they support individuals to get to the underlying patterns, assumptions and beliefs informing their behavior. Whilst I am meeting them in a professional context where they want to grow and develop their careers, invariably this work touches all areas of their lives.

How working with the inner judge was beneficial for me

Before any of my learning in the area of the superego was helpful in my professional context with clients, it was of course most helpful to me. It provided revelations of who I am, how I came to be who I portray, and dispelled many myths, legends, assumptions and beliefs I had long held dear as integral identifiers of me in the world. As my awareness of my 'inner judge' grew, so too did my ability to see more fully how I operate, and with that understanding allow and accept, and decide what to change with much greater self-assuredness and confidence. I have found it confronting and surprising that so much of my behavior and relating have contributed to me living a more confined life – suppressing that which might not be met with approval. Gradually I am identifying elements of my inner judge. Realizing I have absorbed and play out elements/attitudes/ assumptions/patterns of my parents which I had always promised myself I would vehemently reject (I would never be like them in that way) is confronting. I feel more open, and I have discovered a different, more gentle humanity in me which I can meet rather than run from. Realizing I have deluded myself feels vulnerable and open which, once I was able to accept that, opened the way for me to be much more gentle with myself, and consequently with other people too.

I had been (and still am sometimes) great at setting standards about the right way to do things, about what success is, about what is good enough, and then being disappointed, judgmental and angry with the world and others when they (in my perception) didn't meet those standards and approaches to work or life. I had set myself up for a life of disappointment. Though the revelations are sometimes raw and can be painful, I am always in awe at what they reveal. The more deeply I understand them and am curious about them, the more I am intrigued by the complex interrelationships. As I come to be aware of these, I am amazed at how much protection drops away and is no longer needed for me to engage with the world. And engaging with the world in a less defensive way allows me more freedom to express myself fully.

How this is relevant in executive coaching and career development

In the work I do with executives, developing their careers, I am struck that at some point each ambitious, driven, talented person I meet comes to a point of realization. For a continuing successful career they will need to learn new ways. There comes a point of development which is the realization that 'What got me here will not sustain me further in this career', and a fundamental transformation needs to take place. If they continue to suppress so much of who they are, they may fail to progress further. For many this is the point at which their career plateaus.

This transition point is significant for executive development for two reasons:

1. To keep suppressing absorbs so much effort/energy that they don't have the capacity to take on the bigger roles. It is not sustainable.
2. The complexity of the challenges in global corporate life are met more effectively by someone who is prepared to say 'I don't know; however, I have the confidence that we can find a way.'

It has been my experience that those executives who embrace self-awareness with the intent to become better leaders make this transition. And it is through understanding their patterns, assumptions, judge and mask that they are able to do this. As they open and allow more of who they truly are to be expressed, they become more visionary leaders, more able to engage their teams to the vision required to respond to global business challenges.

Self-inquiry – the key for me

About the same time as I was introduced to the work with the superego, I signed up for the Satori Awareness Intensive. The intensive is a week-long experience of self-inquiry. Self-inquiry is a dynamic process that can take us outside our 'comfort zone', opening spaces that can lead to profound and immediate understandings that would not be possible using linear logic. I found that self-inquiry substantially accelerated my self-awareness and understanding of the mask, the superego and inner judge. It absolutely opened my awareness and experience of life. My first Awareness Intensive Retreat was so enlivening – I chewed on, acted out, screamed, shouted, wept, loved, laughed, played, manipulated, enjoyed, relished and deeply explored 'Who is in?' and love, sexuality and beauty. I had never experienced a space that felt so free, so supportive, or that so allowed me to be. It was a joy that through that process I found elements of me I had never given awareness to. It was a revelation coming to know the vastness of how much more I could explore of life and myself rather than the narrow compartments I had so far experienced.

And though that revelation seemed simple and obvious at the time, changing my experience on a day-to-day basis once I returned home did not feel so easy. I returned from Satori, and for the next two weeks maintained the lovely aliveness I'd experienced there. And then a kind of lostness set in. I felt fearful – didn't feel the least bit inquisitive, except on an intellectual level – which provided a marvelous shield of defense to protect me from deeply being with the lostness. In the meantime I went to work, I engaged with my friends as I always had, and felt a deep brewing dissatisfaction with it all. What I wanted to do was drop it all and explore more deeply.

In October of that year I attended a two-week Satori, this time in Corfu. I yearned to explore more deeply, having a strong sense that what I had so far explored had 'hardly scratched the surface'.

I immersed myself and so many defenses immediately showed themselves: fear and resistance, inner rage, self-loathing and anger, to what felt like a point of madness. I felt the insanity of living with conflicting beliefs and assumptions. There was this furious energy of my blood pumping and pounding through my body with intensity such that I felt I would burst. This seemed to be the effort of withholding expression – anger, fear, frustration, love, lust and confusion – the effort of wanting to maintain an outer calm. One lunchtime, feeling desperate and exasperated, I went to sit on the cliff and watch the sea, and what I experienced was inseparable from my inner experience. Below me was the ocean, with waves crashing into each other and the frothy fury of the water moving, swirling and raging. That was me and my experiences and feelings exploding with an inner rage, a boiling sea.

During this time I was also aware of a deep inner voice unambiguously declaring and repeating, 'You have no defenses against the truth of who you are.' Overnight my dreams also echoed with 'You have no defenses against the truth of who you are.' The images, feelings and experiences I met and discovered through inquiry confirmed that 'I have no defenses against the truth of who I am.' And yet, there my defenses were – represented in the pain and tightness, and fear and paranoia and rigidity I was experiencing. My body ached all over with the holding on and holding in, my head pounded, my heart raced. I felt a deep primal fear, feeling like I had the adrenaline of hunted prey rushing through my system, as the creature realizes it is about to die. I realized I felt damaged, unloved, abandoned, raw and open. And I experienced life more gloriously than I ever had before.

As these defenses showed themselves, and the boiling ocean began to settle, I realized many other experiences – a deep stillness and connection at times, and a quiet, sacred space of nothingness. Beauty, intimacy and desire showed themselves. One day I was exploring life and was on the cusp of the familiar fear which would usually have me run and hide. In that moment I clarified my intention and I experienced life so gloriously, wonderfully and joyfully that I fell into a deep shock at the wonder of it all. At another time the experience of life allowed the most sparkling energetic opening of my being: sublime, delicate, intimate, sensuous and delightful.

I left that Awareness Intensive with a conflicting range of feelings, and also felt deeply connected with my inner compass. I had intensely immersed myself into some of the 'so much more' I had longed to experience.

How does this transform?

So now, three years later, what is different, what has changed, how does this transform?

This work, whether it be understanding the mask or the inner judge, transforms by bringing conscious awareness to the feelings, assumptions, patterns and beliefs that I live from. And once I am aware of these assumptions, patterns and beliefs, I do not need to invest energy in defending them.

From the perspective of my professional life I notice I have discarded many of the structures, courtesies and unwritten rules of that environment. I engage there as I do everywhere – direct, real, humorous, intense and light-hearted; being me. There is less distinction between the 'professional' me and the everyday me. There is a consistency, effortlessness and confidence in my engagement with the world and others.

Helen is a human resources executive with more than 20 years' experience working with the world's leading organizations in the areas of talent management, succession and leadership development, executive coaching, and program design and facilitation. Her clients and employers over this time have included some of the world's leading organizations: ANZ, NAB, IBM, NEC and MSD. She has worked in Australia, Europe, Asia and Africa across the financial services, IT, and pharmaceutical sectors.

Anjee Gitte Carlsen

I still remember when I was 6 or 7 years old and my father told me that both God and Jesus could not only always see what I did, but could also read my thoughts (especially the bad ones). From that moment on I prayed endlessly every night, asking forgiveness for my sinful behavior and thoughts.

Often when I was on the point of dropping off to sleep, the memory of another sin would pop into my head and I had to start praying all over again. Today, it really makes me sad to think of that little, innocent girl so adamantly convinced that she was such a bad, evil person.

Of course, this way of looking at myself followed me as I grew up, revealing itself in different areas of my life.

When I was 30 years old it seemed that I had a perfect life: I was working as a schoolteacher, had many close friends, a good relationship and a lovely child.

But I still was not happy. My whole life revolved around being good and doing the right thing, and I didn't even realize I was in a vicious circle, let alone know how to get out of it. And then, one day, I came to the conclusion that I didn't want to spend the rest of my life as I was.

That was when I met the enlightened master Osho. As I looked into his eyes I sensed a feeling of forgiveness: There was the realization that this man was able to love me in spite of all my sins and mistakes. This gave me such hope. Maybe I too would be able to do that one day.

My life changed completely. I got a new name, dropped my schoolteacher job, and moved from Copenhagen to the other side of Denmark, where I joined some others, mostly sannyasins (disciples of Osho) – the group of people who had started the meditation center known as Osho Risk, which still exists today. All my old friends and family thought I was crazy – I was also a little scared myself – because, for the first time, I was doing something wild and unexpected and it felt so good.

This life change and the fact that, later on, I started to work with the inner critic through my own therapy, were big steps in loosening up my structure of self-judgment. And I was so happy to see that we all had the same 'thing' inside. I found I could laugh out loud and have fun, recognizing the stupidity in judging and blaming myself.

I then became a therapist, and continue this work today, giving workshops, sessions and teaching. I am also involved in the running of Osho Risk, which has become quite established. We offer group training, therapist training and Essence training, and there are daily meditations and the gathering of friends.

Four years ago my beloved, Habib, developed a brain tumor. We had been lovers for 10 years and had a beautiful relationship, sharing a house close to Osho Risk.

In the space of one day I was catapulted into complete, total shock in the knowledge that he would soon leave me. During the last year of his life, I devoted all the time I could to Habib.

He had accepted his situation, so we spent most of our time relaxing, sharing each other's company, sitting in the garden, and going to Osho Risk on a daily basis to meditate and hang out with friends.

Surprisingly, it was the most challenging and painful year of my life and yet the most beautiful.

At that point I was still working part time and, to my surprise, one day I realized that the inner criticizing in my sessions and teaching had gone.

No self-blame, no criticism or beliefs that things should have been better or different.

I simply didn't care; there was no space inside me for self-judgment.

I was going through so much in my life, with my beloved dying, that it made such things seem completely meaningless. And my sessions were better than they had ever been. I couldn't believe it and checked it out several times, but the voice of the judge could not be heard. In the beginning I only noticed it in work situations but after a while my peace from self-judgment began to spread throughout my relationships with other people, especially Habib.

I had always believed that if someone close to me should die, then probably I would retreat to the nearest coffee-bar and surrender to my egotism and selfishness (my mother's voice). Instead I relished every precious moment with Habib, taking all kinds of situations on board, totally absorbed in the vastness and depth of this process. There was so much love. And I could love and appreciate myself for just being this.

Habib died at home, the same day and time that Osho had left his body many years before. I don't know why this should have happened, but it was just one of many mysteries unfolding.

There were four of us there the day that Habib left, there was complete silence and light, and he was so happy to be leaving his tired body.

Now nearly three years have passed since Habib's death, and I have had to face the fact that the judge was making a comeback, but in a much milder way than before. I have had a lot of compassion for myself in these last three years, and have been helped by the support of my friends.

Anjee is a Danish teacher and psychotherapist. Currently her work involves a combination of teaching psychology and holding private counseling sessions and courses in Tantra, communication, meditation and inner child. Beside that she is involved in the management of the meditation center, Osho Risk, in Denmark, where she has been living and working for the last 25 years.

Krishnananda and Amana

Working through our depression and self-hatred
Crystal is a 37-year-old woman who appears troubled, anxious,

and depressed. When she talks, she is hesitant and corrects herself repeatedly, looking down and rarely making eye contact. Her energy feels collapsed and hopeless and she has a perpetual sad look on her face. When she shares about herself and her life, it is full of self-judgment and pessimism. Listening to her, it is difficult not to get affected by her heaviness and desperation.

As a child, her mother criticized her continually. She was the second of two girls, and after her mother had her first daughter she did not want any more children. But when she became pregnant with Crystal, she reluctantly gave birth but resented caring for her. As she grew up, her mother continually found fault with her and compared her endlessly to her older sister. Her father was too absent and collapsed to defend her against her mother's attacks and abuse.

Crystal's relationships with men have ended in her being rejected because she was told that she is too needy and depressed. This only confirms her already negative self-image and sadness. She says that she feels lonely in her life and desperately wants to find a man to be with. She lacks the insight that from this space, she will only create more rejection.

Our work with Crystal has been a gradual process of teaching her how to get some space from her massively tyrannical inner judge and delicately reflecting her essential qualities. She has never been close to someone who did not judge or reject her. We have needed to deflect her constant insistence on getting quick solutions for her unhappiness but we have acknowledged her desperation and her pain and explained that any effective solution requires a different approach.

Instead, we have listened to her steady incessant stream of negative self-judgments with patience, space, and compassion, and helped her to understand why she is so hard on herself. Crystal's is a clear case of what we call 'type 1 depression', coming from an out-of-control inner critic. It always comes from the deep trauma of being shamed and abused as a child. She needs immense patience and love.

Periods of depression and self-hatred can be highly challenging for all of us. By definition, when we are depressed, we lack life energy and vitality, have little motivation to change, lack self-esteem, are full of mistrust, and usually have a negative and even cynical view of life. In some cases we may talk slowly, with little energy, and may even have periods of silence between words. Our movements may be lethargic and in general it can feel that it takes much effort to express any energy at all.

Perhaps it may be surprising to say, but depression is a defense, a defense against feeling pain and fear. It is perhaps more difficult to see that this is really a defense because the feelings seem so authentic and real. But depression can be so chronic and difficult to penetrate and heal because there is no movement of energy, and nothing heals without movement. When we are depressed, we may believe that we are feeling pain. But not really. (One way to know that it is a defense is that when you are with a person who is depressed, there is an instinct and intuition inside of you that wants to shake the person, wants to wake him up and move something.)

Most of us go through periods of feeling discouraged, unmotivated, and negative about ourselves, our life, and life in general. The question is how resilient we are, how quickly it takes us to recover from a setback, how inspired we are about our life, and how much of our time we spend being negative. In some ways, we all walk a tightrope between positivity and negativity. It is a constant challenge to find meaning in life that sustains us and to persevere in spite of the difficulties in life. We may have had periods in our life when we could not bring ourselves out of negativity, when our shame is so deep that it is basically sabotaging our love life, creativity, and/or health. Those are the times when we may have needed to reach out for help.

Depression has different forms and it is good to know which form we are dealing with in ourselves or in others.

- Type 1: This is a **continual attack from an inner judge that is out of control**. This attack can come in the form of outer criticism or inner voices. Often this kind of attack can be chronic, resulting in a baseline of depression in a person's life. Other times, it is more acute.
- Type 2: Another cause is when **we are not acting or living our life in a way that is in harmony with our potential, integrity, and inner wisdom**.
- Type 3: A third cause is when we **cannot forgive ourselves for something we have done that has been hurtful to others or ourselves**.
- Type 4: A fourth cause of depression is when we **cannot recover from a rejection, a financial setback, a loss of a loved one, or creative failure**.

All four of these causes are deeply related but it is helpful in working with depression and self-hatred to isolate each one. There is also some evidence to suggest that depression has a biological cause, and medication can be a valuable and necessary resource for some of us with depression. It is important for you to consider and sometimes use it.

We will seek out a therapist when our pain has reached a critical point, when our compensations are no longer working, and/or when our self-judgments are controlling our life. Often we may have become desperate and perhaps even suicidal. But sometimes, we are not aware that we are depressed because our low energy, hopelessness, and negativity may be chronic. We may not know any other state of being. Either way, we may need someone to help us solve our problems, to help find relief from our pain, and to discover another way of living.

The work
We would like to describe our work with Crystal as a guide to how to deal with our own periods of depression and self-hatred.

1. Healing with the heart

She clearly has type 1 depression. The cornerstone of our work with her meant becoming her heart energy. This did not mean heaping praise on her, because that does little good. It meant that we have been a source of kind support and love she did not get. We are reflecting with our energy, our heart, even with words, her beauty, uniqueness, and specialness. Our role as her therapists has been to **replace her negative self-image by providing her with the love, support, guidance, acceptance, and ability to recognize her specialness that she missed**. Slowly, as she begins to bring our love inside, **positive impressions replace the negative ones**.

2. Explaining what depression is and where it comes from

We also needed to explain to Crystal why she was feeling so bad about herself and life. The experience of depression is basically a **disconnection from ourselves**. It is a very convincing state of trance in which we are not in touch with the natural flow of our life energy, creativity, contribution, and being part of a greater wholeness and connection with existence. This can be an acute or chronic state.

The love of self does not come from accomplishments, status, or image. All of this can vanish in a moment and quite often depression hits when these substitutes fail. Love of self comes from a state of connection, an inner experience that is not dependent on any support or reflection from the outside. It comes from being loved, appreciated, and respected as a child and having this body and soul memory deep inside as we grow older.

When we miss this basic 'love food', we develop a self-concept in which we feel like a bad person. Furthermore, because of the deprivation we received, we may act in ways that are clinging, collapsed, aggressive, demanding, unkind, irresponsible, and destructive because we feel so empty inside. Then our behavior reaffirms the belief that we are basically bad. It all comes from the hurt inside from not being loved. We lost the connection to the natural beauty and specialness inside of us.

3. Teaching about the judge

Depression, low energy, and lack of hope come from attacks of our inner judge. Crystal believed that this is her natural state because she felt basically defective and deficient inside. She did not understand that it had its roots in her negative experiences in childhood that now live in the violence of the attacks of their inner judge. Furthermore, she also did not understand that healing could happen by learning to deal with this judge in the way that we would guide her.

We also needed to teach her about the judge. We explained that this part of the person's psyche came into existence to carry the verbal and non-verbal messages from her parents and culture to teach her how she should be, think, behave, and feel. But often the messages she received were abusive, full of expectations, pressure, and judgments that had nothing to do with who she was or is. She was harshly criticized, humiliated, punished, or physically abused and the mother put her own guilt and lack of fulfillment on her. We become deeply infected with this pressure and guilt.

We have no defenses against this kind of conditioning. We are helpless and unaware that the parents and culture are often misguided and unconscious. What originated from the outside in the form of rules, standards, expectations and pressure gets internalized, as we get older. Then we no longer need outside regulation; **it moves inside in the form of our inner judge.** Normally, we respond in one of two ways to the dictates of our outer and inner judge. We try to meet the expectations as best as we can, pushing ourselves to perform and be the person we are expected to be. We may succeed and become the way the parents and the culture expect. But later, we may burn out, get ill, have an accident, suffer from a failure, or have a crushing realization that we have not been living our own life. We find ourselves lost, alone, frightened, and guilty.

Another way we respond to our conditioning is to collapse into feeling inferior, defective, and eventually, depressed. We sink into the belief that we will never make it or never be good enough so what is the use of even trying. Rarely, we may rebel against these pressures, standards, and rules but even then, the judge still has the power because we are reacting against the judge.

When we are being run by our inner judge (or by the rules, standards, and opinions of others), we are not learning to trust our own intelligence.

How we get distance from the judge
One way is **connecting with the pain and the rage** under the depression for being conditioned in a way that was rigid, unloving, unsupportive, and perhaps violent.

The second is learning how to **listen to another voice inside**, one that comes from love, from the heart, and from a space of wisdom. This voice supports the natural flow of life and the sense of purpose and relaxed connection to the greater meaning of our life. Eventually, we can teach the client to connect to this inner guidance on his or her own through the practice of meditation.

Identifying the voices of the judge
Regardless of which type of depression it is, it is important to identify how the judge is attacking us. This may not be obvious and it often helps to suggest some statements that you feel your judge is saying. In the case of type 1 depression, the voices may be very old and familiar. In the other cases, they may be newer and less familiar. You might ask yourself:

'What is my judge actually saying to me – that I am a horrible person? Or useless, incapable, insensitive, unlovable, unkind...'

'Is there someone in my life today that is saying the same thing?'

'What happens to me when I hear this inner voice?'

'How do I feel in my body?'

'What happens to my energy?'

'What do I think about myself when I hear these judgments?'

'Do I compare myself?'

'Do I agree? Do I fight back?'

'How do I behave when I hear these judgments?'

'Do I give up? Try harder? Go to some addiction?'

Trace the voices back to the source
Next, it is helpful to see if these voices originated from childhood, and if so, when and under what circumstances. Often they come from a parent who was critical and full of high expectations. Sometimes they come from comparison to a sibling or classmates. Sometimes they come from how our parents responded to mistakes or poor performance. Or they can come from a general feeling of high standards and rigidity in the home environment. Other times, they come from deeper traumas such as physical or emotional abuse or neglect from a parent.

Feeling the impact of the attack
At this point, it is important to explore experientially the impact that the judge has on you. One simple way to do this is to place a cushion in front of you and ask yourself to imagine that it is your judge (or it can represent your father or your mother if they were one of the sources of the judge).

Then say to yourself some of the judgments coming from this energy and see how it feels in the body. Imagine yourself as a child and ask how this is for a small, innocent, receptive, and trusting child.

You can ask yourself:

'What happens to my energy when I feel this attack?'

'How do I feel about myself when I feel this attack?'

'What happens to my self-confidence?'

'Are these judgments attacking me all the time or only when I get rejected, fail, etc.?'

'On a scale from 1 to 10, 10 being the strongest, how much do I believe that these judgments are true?'

'Can I see how these early judgments have affected my life?'

Most often, an attack from the judge puts us into a combination of deep insecurity, feelings of inadequacy, and shame, but also it can put us into shock. Shock causes us to freeze, become confused, and unable to feel. We become emotionally and physically paralyzed.

You can ask:

'What happens in my body when I feel this attack?'

'Am I able to feel my body?'

'Can I think clearly or do I get confused?'

'Perhaps I am not able to feel or say anything?'

Changing channels

Changing channels is the term we use for teaching us how to listen to a different inner voice inside. The voice of the inner judge comes with harshness, often impatience, and merciless condemnation. It is the inner voice that we have learned to listen to and also attract from other people because of our negative conditioning. But had we been raised in a way that was supportive, loving, caring, teaching us to accept mistakes as an opportunity to learn, and gently and strongly guiding us to discover our potential, we would have a less critical inner judge. However, now in our life, we can learn to tune in to this other voice – one that is compassionate.

We can pick a situation that has provoked a judge attack. First, identify the judge voices and then feel the effect. On a separate cushion, you can ask yourself to imagine that this is a totally different energy, one that can see the situation clearly but give you feedback about it that is guiding, loving, and supportive, one where you can learn from the situation and grow. We call this '**the voice of the heart**', or '**the voice of the loving wisdom**'.

You can hear the voice of the heart by using your own intuition to evaluate the situation and see what this energy would say as a way of being supportive, clear, and guiding. It takes time and practice for us to learn to switch channels, especially when we are triggered. In those moments naturally the judge voice will come. It takes a conscious effort to switch channels.

Risk

Sometimes we are depressed and hate ourselves when we are not following or living our truth. The judge may be indicating the need to take a step. The problem is that the judge does it in such a way that all we feel is wrong, bad, incapable, or unforgivable. But a step is needed to help us come back to life. In these cases, it is helpful to find what the step could be. Explore your fears around taking this step and perhaps some baby steps in the direction of doing it.

Let's look at some examples of risk:

Engage yourself in **activities that bring a quality of dignity and self-love** and help to connect with essence. This can include anything that helps connect with genuine joy, creativity, curiosity, and life energy, such as dance classes or other classes that inspire creativity, physical exercise on a regular basis, learning and taking steps toward developing a career and so on. Another risk could be to **set a limit** or **separate** from a parent or people in your life who are supporting the judge.

The risk can be taking steps to self-actualize. Because of the judge, you may have collapsed or sabotaged efforts to discover and live your gifts. Discover what your passions are and help yourself to take small steps in the direction of living it.

A risk might be to apologize to the person you have hurt. If you are having trouble recovering from a rejection, a financial failure, or loss, the risk could be to understand what you can **learn from the experience**, to ask yourself why it might have happened for you to grow, and to feel the grief of the loss or failure. Eventually, you can put the pieces together by dealing with the shame and the abandonment wounds.

Meditation to connect with the inner wisdom
In a natural relaxed state, we can make the connection to the natural flow of our life energy. But often, when we are depressed and self-critical we are too overtaken by the voice of the inner judge to feel this connection. You can use meditation to reconnect. Here is an example of this kind of meditation:

'Take some moments to relax and go inside.

Taking a deep breath and gently allowing your attention to come inside...

Observing your breath, observing your body, and allowing the natural flow of the breath to take you deeper inside, more and more relaxed...

Deeper and deeper, more and more relaxed...

Begin by noticing and hearing the voice of this inner judge that is so critical.

Observe the voices of criticism – do this, don't do this, you should do this, how could you be so stupid, you will never make it, and so on.

Feel the effect of this criticism. Feel how it makes you feel in the body. Feel how it makes you feel about yourself, how it affects your energy and your enthusiasm.

Notice how often this voice attacks you, how long it has attacked you. Notice how it attacks you right now in your life.

Now, let it go. Imagine that it is fading away into the background.

Allow yourself to tune in to the area of your heart.

Feel the natural loving energy that comes from the heart.

Let that energy spread all through your body.

Allow yourself to sink deeply into this loving energy.

From this space, you can know that all that is true is that you are here to find your own special beauty.

You are here to discover your own gifts, your own unique contribution, and your natural flow.

To find what makes your heart sing. To be yourself, to find yourself. To be part of the wonderful flow of life, in your own special way.

Along the way, you may make mistakes; you may encounter challenges, and obstacles. That is part of the process.

Keep going but go with this gentle loving energy, easy, relaxed, and flowing.

Relax and enjoy the gentle unfolding of your true self.

Don't push. But persevere. Listen to your heart. It will guide you. It will help you find your own way.

Relax and feel the natural flow of life and of your life.

Remember, the heart, not the mind, will bring you home.

Remember this space. It is always there. It just takes a little effort to focus here and not on the voice of your judge.

Remember to listen to your heart.

And now, whenever you are ready, you can slowly allow yourself to come back.

Take a deep breath and, whenever you like, you can open your eyes and be back.'

Conclusion

We have all experienced being judged and rejected. What we need most of all is compassionate acceptance and listening to our pain. We can easily become obsessed and even indulge in ruminating about how horrible we are, how much a failure, how unlovable we are, and how terrible life is.

At some point, we will need to step in and redirect this focus. But it is also not enough just to listen compassionately and patiently and to understand our pain. We also need to switch channels to learn to listen to 'the loving voice' as an antidote to our judge. We also need to slowly and gradually give ourselves small assignments that build our resources and self-confidence.

Depression and self-hatred is simply a misunderstanding, as if we are listening to the wrong TV channel. Perhaps we have listened to this channel all of our lives or perhaps, because of a recent rejection or failure, this channel has taken over all the other wavelengths. But by following the steps we have outlined, we can bring ourselves back home to appreciating our lives, our beauty, our gifts, and the splendor of being alive.

Krishnananda and Amana are the founders and directors of The Learning Love Institute, Sedona, Arizona, USA and authors of several books.

Jayana

Coming to understand how the inner judge has been controlling my life has been a tremendous gift. But first it really pissed me off.

My first contact was in a Satori meditation retreat. Having a healthy ego, I was shocked to my core to discover I had been controlled, rewarded, and emotionally castrated all my life by this internal monster. I was determined to learn everything I could to shut it up, kill it off and 'get on with my enlightenment'. What a joke.

It permeated all my relationships, my work life, how I loved my children, how deeply I doubted myself, even where I chose to live. It was everywhere. The rose-colored glasses were off. I needed help! It was like the movie *Alien*. This thing was inside me, part of my system, I couldn't run away from it or ignore it, and it had been making my life hell.

I also began to see how this judge was familiar. My pushy attempts to succeed, my crushing defeats and depression. I began to see the source of my low self-esteem, the self-rejection, health issues, isolation, recurring insane drivenness. Everything was measured, right or wrong – I had become right or wrong.

Mostly wrong. And the fatigue. Endless.

Help came with a teacher. Decision time. I committed to stick to this, no matter what. Meeting others in groups brought shared insights and gave me hope. There is another way to be in life. Practice of techniques learnt, highs and lows, laughter and tears, getting lost, finding my way, growing in resilience, learning to support myself, moving this into my daily life. Hit the fast-forward button: I bumped into another layer called the Enneagram, an ancient system revealing how nine core personality types are expressed in our life. This opened up another can of worms, literally. Now I saw not only my own, but everyone else's craziness. Get me out of here! I realized I could not turn away, or go back. It would be walking away from myself, my very life. The worms were already inside anyway. The only way out is through.

I saw how both fit together, inner judge as a steel fist and the Enneagram as the glove. I realized I could fiddle about with the Enneagram for years in endless distraction, missing, acting unconsciously, then let my inner judge beat me up about this as well, unless I dealt directly with the fist inside.

It's through experience (by repeated failures and experiment) that I recommend it's necessary to get very clear with the inner judge work first. Once you have solid ground, it's a natural evolution to refine this with learning your own habits of acting out through your Enneatype.

The inner judge is most of the time telling us we are wrong; it uses anything and everything. It uses the Enneagram information too. In fact a huge amount of ammunition to throw mud-pies at us comes from this material if we are not aware. That is where I got lost for some time, and see others wandering around still 'keeping busy'.

This has been the purest of adventures. No book or movie thriller has equaled it.

I am opening as myself, exploring creativity, letting go of

ideas of who I thought I had to be to have love and approval, and to survive. Most were big, fat, fake lies. Life is supporting me in ways I could never have imagined.

Sharing this work as a teacher now is another evolution. I feel incredibly grateful to my beloved teacher and friend Avikal, for his patience, directness to cut to the truth, and great love in lighting the way.

Jayana is mother, partner, visual art maker, inner judge and Enneagram teacher.

Yeshua Marco Firinu

Some time ago a journalist from a major magazine about tattoos contacted me for an article. It was an old friend, so we decided to find the easiest and most informal way to write the article together: she would send me the questions so I could reply to them in my own time. I got down to responding to each question, writing about my experiences, until I came to a question regarding how and when my story as an artist began, where my love of design, painting and art in general came from. Suddenly, I felt stuck and unable to give an immediate answer, so I began to think about the people to whom I should give merit for my passion, my profession, my success. I ran through the memories of all my high school favorites: the linguistic inventiveness of Magritte, the metaphysics of De Chirico, the sensual and pagan fascination of French 'Pompier', the passionate violence of Tiziano, Boccioni's energy, the exaggerated detail of the Flemish, but even greater than the wonder aroused in me by those works by the great masters – whether old, classic or modern – I remained fascinated by those 'marks' made out on paper. In short I was considering all the things that had impassioned, engaged and nourished me. All of them had a share in my experience, my memories, all of them played a part in my sensi-bility even now; they were the roots from which I had developed my artistic being and way of practicing art. But I wasn't able to really find a starting point. Also when I went even further back, into the memories of when I was a boy, there wasn't a definite beginning, a 'big bang' that could make me shout out: Here it is! That was the moment! At a certain point, in the middle of this examination, all of a sudden some very clear images appeared, fully lit, radiant, full of happiness and emotion, and gradually everything became clear; my past was explained and reformulated in front of me: my story as an artist had begun when I was very little.

My father would leave home early in the morning, often leaving me messages on the bedside table; they were little drawings with wording in speech bubbles. I still remember, with a certain amount of emotion, the marvel that I felt when I saw those designs. There were various subjects done in a simple but decisive way: a man sitting at a table with a full stomach letting me and mum know he couldn't get back for lunch that day and telling us not to worry, that he would have plenty to eat; and then in another, seagulls flying over the sea; or perhaps funny things such as little guys who looked lost and were wandering about in the middle of apartment buildings. My most vivid memory is that of a bunny rabbit. I gazed at it admiringly: I was face to face with an astonishing magic that sprang from those sketches, done with just a few strokes of the pen, but illustrating the subject perfectly. They were about reality but they were something different to reality; they captured and explained it without revealing the mystery, they triggered my imagination and curiosity. It, and they, were marvelous; I was fascinated, and still today the memory brings me happiness, joy, powerful feelings – even now while I am writing, I can feel a particular emotion moving and rising like a wave in my stomach, encircling my neck and making my eyes wet. From those drawings I perceived (even though instinctively) the attention, care and love of that marvelous and magical god who, in the eyes of a child, was my father.

Perhaps this memory didn't remain present afterwards, but I believe it worked in an unconscious way, and contributed to giving me strong motivation and certainty; the fact was I began to be appreciated and praised at school for my ability to design. I sketched a lot – it was one of my favorite pastimes – and slowly as I was growing up, my attention shifted to ever more complicated and detailed subjects: I drew complicated battle scenes with soldiers, aircraft, army vehicles, ships; I knew every airplane model from the Second World War perfectly and I drew them flawlessly in minute detail. Racing cars excited me – the engines, complicated and enticing, mechanisms rich in detail, the people and their expressions. It was a world I entered into and lost myself in, oblivious to the passing of time, and it was full of satisfaction and fun.

In the meantime the moment to leave school arrived and I had to begin thinking about what studies to follow. Apart from my ability to draw, I had no real idea of what I could do. Instead my father, who was a technician for a national telephone company, had ideas that were very precise with regard to my future: 'You should do technical studies,' he said to me. 'In this way I can help you to study and get into the workplace.'

I could sense his affectionate urge, towards me and towards a profession that was also his passion, and his desire to pass this on to me. I remember when I was young, he would spend his free time building equipment – simple radios from scratch – that now and then exploded into a cloud of smoke, to the amusement of all the family and neighbors. But gradually he got better and better until he was able to build powerful stereo amplifiers for record players which, as well as being functional, were also extremely beautiful, carefully designed right down to the last detail. He built the furniture that housed them, loudspeakers, choosing refined materials, good quality wood, leather, velvet, metal borders. As soon as he finished one he sold it so he could make another bigger, more powerful and more beautiful one. Each time, I was spellbound, once again, like when I had been a small child, astounded by his ability, his wonderful sense of taste, the elegance and beauty that emanated from his creations. Then one day he also built me a guitar; he bought a handle from a carpenter, and after having studied a carpentry manual, very slowly and meticulously he built the sound box. Obviously, in the end, it was incredibly beautiful. He had chosen two types of different-coloured wood – there were two gradations that went from dark brown to light golden-brown – its sound was warm and deep, and with the utmost joy I began to strum away and to learn those first fundamental chords. I would then meet up with my friends, in the house of one or another, to play and sing the songs we were able to perform, and my friends were jealous of my beautiful guitar.

However, in the end, my father's will prevailed and I enrolled at the Technical Institute. I didn't have a real urge or passion for it, but deep down I thought it was the right thing to do: the wisest choice; it would make my father happy and would avoid any friction at home.

The Technical Institute was a huge building with four floors; it was an all-boys' school. I found it to be sad; the walls were gray, just like the atmosphere that I breathed, my performance was very poor, there were few things that interested me, I had a hard job studying and my marks were always on the low side. At that time my father continually scolded and punished me, and the tension between us grew day by day.

During the lessons I spent a large part of the time secretly drawing or looking at the top floor of the school where the Artistic High School was. I spied on those boys and girls; I caught glimpses of them behind the windows, designing, making models, painting. I was envious of them; they looked happy and absorbed in what they were doing, in contrast to me. I continued to become more depressed and disinterested. The wish to dedicate myself to artistic studies began to get clearer. At the beginning it was a sort of forbidden desire. The fear of telling my father prevented me from thinking about it seriously. I would have had to face him, in the knowledge that I had deluded him, betraying his trust, losing his support – in short, his love. Inside I felt myself collapsing, with no strength to fight. I felt like death, I felt I couldn't tell him and, above all, I couldn't have sustained the confrontation that would have followed.

In the meantime the situation continued to get worse; my school performance was terrible and my relationship with my father continued to become even more of a disaster. Scolding, demands, arguments made up my life and my unbearable family relationships. Things finally came to a head one evening when I was faced with a series of bad marks and a detrimental note from my teachers. In a spurt of anger my father destroyed the guitar he had made for me and tore down all the posters in my room. The atmosphere was terrible, especially in the evenings when he arrived home, pre-warning me of his tension with long silences and penetrating stares: my body would go rigid and I couldn't feel my genitals anymore; it was like everything inside had frozen. My shoulders were tense, and I had the sensation that my sight had become restricted; it was as if I was wearing blinkers, like the ones horses wear so they can't see to the sides.

The image I had of myself was that of a young boy who wasn't very bright, who was ugly, rough, didn't give a damn and who was deceiving and betraying the trust of his parents. Repressing the pain from this situation with food, I stupefied myself by eating a lot, above all in the evening when we were together at home, but it didn't work very well and I continued to feel more and more guilty. Then one day I plucked up the courage to tell my father something that a few months previously would have seemed impossible to say: that what I really wanted to do was artistic studies.

A period began that was even worse than before; arguments, tensions and disputes became continuous. According to my father it was an absurd and reckless idea; our family wasn't well off enough to be able to support me in long life-experiments. He thought they were just the eccentric ideas of an inexperienced boy who didn't have the slightest idea of how one had to make a living and said that I needed to 'get my head put right' and think about studying in order to find a job and support a family; in short, do what everyone does, underlining that 'everyone' was intended as meaning normal people. The thought of not being able to survive economically, faced by the hardship of life, terrorized me; I was afraid of becoming a tramp, or in the best hypothesis, that I would end up doing a makeshift job. I was divided and at odds with myself. Deep down I felt he had a point; what's more, I feared that he might be right! A sense of guilt continued to plague me and for this reason I stopped arguing in order to appease my father, and for the time being I renounced my own ambitions. But it was impossible for me to imagine myself continuing my studies in such a sad and somber direction – one that made me feel like I was dead – in the light of what I had begun to imagine, which made me feel happy and full of life and light.

In the end my father gave up; he had probably also been advised and convinced by relatives or professors, and so, completely against his will, he gave his consent under one condition: he would let me withdraw from the Technical Institute to enrol at the Artistic High School, only if I got a job and worked until the beginning of the new scholastic year. And so it was: I worked all summer, skipping the holidays, but if that was the price to be paid, it didn't matter, I was happy. I really was a young boy who wanted to be 'good' and to please his parents and perhaps, in order to alleviate my sense of guilt a little, it seemed only right to give them all of my salary. This made me feel good; I had an image of myself that was 'grown-up', more adult; I felt I had a clean conscience. Now I know that at the time I was only paying tribute to my inner judge to keep it quiet and leave me in peace.

I gave myself a few things, like the first LP that I bought with my own money. It was the first record I had ever owned, and I listened to it on our very powerful stereo at home; the title was prophetic: *Axis: Bold as Love* by Jimi Hendrix. It was shortly after this that I began to experience the boldness of love.

On my first day of school at the Artistic High School I was excited and full of enthusiasm. It was a pleasant autumnal day; everything was beautiful, the school was bright, the corridors were furnished with stunning plaster moldings by major artists. I felt great, my male companions were great, and my female companions even more so; everything had a beautiful smell of plaster, of carbon paper; I was among people who were like me – we had the same ideas and aspirations. The teachers were artistic and told us about their lives, sharing their experiences and their craft. Each story was different from the last, with different personalities and emotions, but they all had the same effect on me: they set me off on a journey in my imagination; to me they were fascinating stories of adventure and the love of art, love expressed in many different ways, even through difficulty and adversity. They made me dream and to want my life to be like it had been for them; fascinating, adventurous, with the opportunity for self-exploration.

Life at the high school was a leisurely downhill run nearly all the way. I don't remember any particular problems, I didn't have to put in too much effort, and my results were very good, particularly in artistic subjects where I attracted praise from the teachers. Above all, I had no fears for the future, perhaps due to a touch of naiveté or madness (as my father put it), but probably because I really felt at home.

As soon as school finished I was taken on as an assistant at the very same high school and shortly after I became a teacher. My salary enabled me to be self-sufficient, to follow my studies at the Academy of Fine Arts, and to dedicate myself to my profession, fulfilling my wish to express myself and to explore the arts. My father became more relaxed towards me; the worry over my survival had disappeared and the tension had been shifted to other matters (it was the time of the student riots and great social change, and due to my restlessness I had no trouble throwing myself into difficult situations and was able to give my parents good reasons for worrying; my urge for autonomy was getting ever stronger and more decisive). But in general everything went well between us, and I noted the interest he took in my progress; he helped me by building furniture for the studio and once more, once again, I could perceive the magic of his elegance and refinement. Every time I stop to think about it, a sense of gratitude floods over me; it fills me with joy and wonder at the enormous support I received from his existence.

In my life I have never had a real problem to survive and I have always made enough to live, doing what I like to do, things connected to my vision, often achieving a certain amount of success.

Soon after, my father passed away, suddenly and very prematurely, right in the middle of my rebellious stage, leaving me with an enormous emptiness, but enabling me to really take responsibility for the life I was living. I didn't have to answer to anyone's expectations anymore and I could make my own decisions. Now, years later, with the knowledge that I have acquired on the inner judge, the image of my father/superego has fallen away and his memory is permeated with tenderness and humanity. Now and then, especially at night, on my own and far from my daily obligations, I sit down and dedicate some time to meditation and I see that he is still alive in me. Memories emerge and tears trickle, purifying the connection I feel with his humanity, his way of being, strong, intelligent and sensitive and, through learning from many mistakes and difficulties, his capacity to share the fun and beauty he carried in his heart.

I think the role he has played in my life is priceless, from the seeds he scattered, subsequently generating and allowing for the development of my potential. Even when going against my decisions, in our disagreements, I feel he has strengthened me; through rebellious conflict he taught me to assert myself and this has enabled me to define myself as an individual. Even at this moment I can feel his love.

Now that I am also a father, I look at my children; I watch them when they go head to head with the image of me as their inner judge. It's not always easy for me to help them with their suffering; I can't always find a way to make them understand and accept the rules and ways that will help them to navigate socially and to survive. I don't have a magic wand or a ready solution in my hand. I stop, I listen to them, I feel their hearts, their vulnerability; I also let my heart open up, allowing myself to be more vulnerable and soft. Often in those moments I can sense their souls, which, like a perfume, expand and reach out to me. Now my wish is to also reach out to them, to make them feel loved, to discover something beautiful and productive like that bunny rabbit my father left on my bedside table; something that meant so much to me. I let my sensitivity and imagination pull the rabbit out of the magician's hat.

It begins in the heart as a spontaneous intuition, like jumping on a train at the last moment, with a little bit of madness and fun. I know I can do it.

I also know that I will not be able to perform the magic if I let myself be weighed down by security, survival and conformity.

'Ongoing evolution' would seem to be the motto that best suits Yeshua Marco Firinu: a creative professional, teacher of the arts, who has gone from painting and design to sculpture, graphics and the computer, creating an enviable wealth of experience. Pioneer and innovator in the ancient, noble art of tattooing in Italy, he is currently exploring new grounds in self-consciousness. He is a disciple of Osho and active member of the Integral Being Institute on work regarding the inner judge. He is father to two children who, together with his

wife, form his tribe.

Liateresa Prada Chiappari

What is the inner judge? For me it is that voice or sensation that, even before opening my eyes in the morning, is already chattering inside my head; it's that mixture of thoughts that tell me how I am and how I feel; it's that mixture of sensations through which I experience the day and which repeat themselves, like a stuck record that keeps going back to the beginning. Recognizing that voice, which for years I believed was my voice and which has directed me in the film which has been my life to date, led to the realization and discovery of a fundamental part of me.

Distinguishing and recognizing that voice and waking up before it does is the center of this work with the inner judge.

This morning I realized that I had made a mistake in my work. Years ago I would have experienced this simple event as an enormous tragedy, with a sense of profound inadequacy and a whole series of fears seasoned with a sense of guilt and anger. I would have immediately looked for a solution so as to not feel frustration and to hide my responsibility: exactly like little children who charge into the table breaking the antique vase, saying 'It fell on me... it wasn't my fault.'

What happened today was that I was able to observe everything that was happening, passing through all these emotions, without remaining hooked on any of them. I have taken responsibility, I have seen my superego at work and I have said, 'It's true, I did make a mistake,' and there was no space for reactivity and automatic defenses as the moment was saturated by my presence and solidity. This is perhaps one of the central changes that I can see, thanks to this process of understanding the inner judge; a process in which I can perceive and recognize the various layers of my personality and how I operate mechanically, and take responsibility.

I often listen to people who say they don't feel good, complain about their lives, their deep unhappiness and the sense of being imprisoned in a repetitive pattern, and at the same time they keep repeating with conviction and enormous pigheadedness, 'This is me; I can't do anything about it!'

This state of resignation keeps us glued to the past, whenever we nurture our unhappiness, and it is, in my experience, one of the most powerful beliefs we are attached to. Believing that we are without hope is the deep core from which my inner judge gains its force.

Even at this moment, it is here constantly judging what I am doing and how I'm doing and noting that, for example, what I'm writing certainly isn't that great, that I could do better and that someone will think I'm ridiculous.

And yet, these thoughts, this voice, are no longer as loud as they were; they are more like a passing cloud, sometimes looming large and threatening, but then moving on, and it is my capacity to be aware that completely lightens and changes my reality. It's no longer a stuck record that keeps going back to the beginning with the same boring song, but a new compilation which even contains unpublished tracks.

The first time that I participated in a workshop on the inner judge, the impression that I had inside and out was of annihilation, as the fog that I was used to having in front of my eyes suddenly vanished. Seeing the reality of how my life worked was an experience that brought total and immediate change: I saw that the part called the superego (inner judge) was everywhere in my daily life, that I was completely conditioned and possessed by this voice that gave me directions and made me do things, feeling and living as it wanted. There wasn't a single truly free moment.

The first fundamental step towards my independence was in the days following the seminar when, for the first time, I became aware of, sensed and recognized the omnipresence of the voice of my judge. That omnipresence showed itself through what I call 'the loop': the activity of an interior dialogue made up of aggression and manipulation on the part of the judge (the parents inside) and reactivity on the part of my ego (the child part in me); this is the prison where I had believed I was safe for most of my life. Associated to this I had an inner image of myself – together with the noise of the dialogue – that I was a giant inside a bullet-proof glass jar.

The subtle boundary line between who I believe I am and who I really feel I am, between the misery of living in a restricted space and the experience of not having boundaries, is determined by my structure: and what I mean is that in reality it is me that creates and sustains the walls of the jar, moving myself with the speed of light from the position of the ego to that of the superego, creating a vortex of such confusion and such noise that the voice of my soul, my true Self, is lost.

In recent years the understanding of how it works has sharpened.

It is like being on the edge of a wood full of different trees and having an appointment somewhere, near an oak tree. The beginning was like this for me, realizing that I was in front of a wood and that there were plants that I didn't know; then I began to distinguish them one by one and, after the initial panic and the fear of not getting to the appointment on time, I began to become aware of my surroundings. I felt curious about what was around me; I began to notice that there was much more than I had realized: flowers, the sky, rocks, scent, moss, shadows and light, the curves of the branches, and many other details.

My sense of haste dwindled and time got longer as arriving for the appointment was no longer that important; **the one I was due to meet was myself.**

I had to deal with a basic concept in my ego, that each piece of my personal past, once seen, felt and digested, could be archived; the thought is: now you can rest, go to sleep, you've been really good – but I now know it doesn't really work like this. In fact, remembering myself and consciously defending myself from the attacks of the inner judge is a practice and fundamental daily exercise; it is through my commitment to staying on guard and alert that I'm able to transform my interior relationship with the judge and recoup vital energy for myself.

Therefore, I go into the wood with a picnic basket, but inside it I also have all the tools I have acquired and that have become personal resources; in this way should the 'bad wolf' come too close and bother me, I can do everything in my power to defend myself.

Today my inner judge is also my inner sage; it is also my journey companion, not just the ear-splitting voice that deafened me, but rather one whom I can decide whether to pay attention to or not.

What has been completely transformed in my life is the relationship that I have with myself; it is the way I see the world and everything that surrounds me, it is how I feel and experience my relationships with my husband and my daughter, my friends and my work, it is the chance to really live in a way with new, unimaginable opportunities inside that glass jar. It is to welcome and support myself in everything I am, to enjoy the journey while I discover this splendid wood and delight in the feeling of the earth beneath my feet and everything around.

A story that I'm very fond of is about the master of a house who sets off on a journey and how, not long after, the servants, convinced he won't come back, begin to believe they are the owners of the house, which results in enormous confusion. Everyone wants and believes that they can take charge but no-one really knows how.

This is exactly what my mind believes, or my emotions or even my body.

But then (I love stories that have a good ending) one day: 'The master of the house comes back and harmony is restored.'

'I'm back.'

For 30 years Liateresa has been working with multinational companies in a commercial context. Contemporarily, 20 years ago, she began looking for something without knowing exactly what it was she was looking for; today she supports people that, like her, are on a journey, whether through superego counseling work, or cranio-sacral bodywork.

Antar Mandir

I'm going to describe something of my transformation and work with my superego. In setting out to do that, I know that I'm embarking on a journey of which I can know very little of the directions I will take nor of the destination. I feel glad to know that, because it fills the first steps of this journey with mystery and excitement. And like any real journey where there is space for adventure, I'm aware that this journey also has its danger. It might sound strange for me to say this – am I writing about a subject I am familiar with, or not? I would hope so, and yet this is a very special subject, and not at all like some other subject of which I could write and feel quite confident of what I know. For example, I have been a violin maker for the past 25 years, so I could write about violins with ease – their history, construction, the wealth of lore which surrounds them, even how to play them. I could write about psychology, history, cooking, martial arts, parenting, or any of the other things with which I have filled my life, and with any of those subjects I would simply draw upon the facts and impressions in my memory. But this subject is different. A catalogue of meditations done, of workshops, seminars, trainings and retreats completed, of insights gained and spiritual experiences 'experienced' would say very little of where I am now, or who I have become.

This is such a tricky place, attempting to discuss my inner work. I contemplate what to write, and I want to impress you. I want to tell the story of how connected and wise I have become.

I want to try to convey the richness of experience that makes my journey so special, the courage I have summoned to face my demons, and the persistence I have exhibited – the hard work. But something feels wrong about that – it doesn't feel good like I thought it would. Oh yes, of course! It's my superego. Oh no, I fell for it again!

Writing from a more humble point of view would do no good. It would simply be my superego wanting to impress with my humility and selflessness. 'Ah, this transformation work has really made an honest and simple man of him' – or so I would think if I were you. 'I really think I would like this guy.' My superego rubs its hands together craftily as it plots my continued survival on the basis of my appeal to others.

As I become aware of my superego and its attempts to control this writing, I'm filled with emotion. I told you this would be dangerous. I'm angry at the attempt to control me, and also filled with sadness and pity. Its plotting and interfering seem well intentioned but pathetic. Underneath all this lie the things that my superego was trying to cover up. I can feel fear in the pit of my stomach: I'm not sure if I have transformed at all. Oh God, what if this is all a delusion? Sometimes I feel like such a beginner, still struggling with many of the same issues that I wanted to resolve years ago.

I'm aware that I'm under attack from my superego. I know because I can feel it in my body. I can feel a defensive coat of armor around me. It protects me but I lose sensitivity. I lose the sensation of being connected with life and the world. It feels terrible, like being shut in a cage – a cage which is pressing hard on me from all sides – but by remembering that it's a superego attack I then have the strange sensation of being outside of the attack looking in. It feels as if a strange displacement of time and space has just happened and for a moment I am left reeling. Without the attitudes and opinions of my superego and of its complementary child I feel confused. I don't seem to know anything or even who I am. This only lasts a second before this place of not-knowing starts to open up and something very precious happens. It feels like freshness, the very essence of a fresh new day, of a delicate and beautiful dawn. Existence seems to invite me to discover, not to know but to discover. All the fear and anxiety is replaced by a simple feeling of presence which by its very nature has integrity. I breathe a breath of relief. I savor this opening of awareness and the goodness with which it is filled. I find all that I need here: respite from the relentless machinations of my superego and insight into the subject that I was writing about.

I only have this to offer. This small precious moment, this possibility of beauty and goodness. It is small and easily missed, but it is so very valuable. Its value is mine, our value is one and the same, and with that knowing I lose all desire to impress the reader. In the place of the desire, perhaps what was always there underneath it, I feel playful and curious. I feel a connection to others which is creative and spontaneous. I want to give and I want to take, like a child who is exuberant at the joy of playing for its own sake.

I feel that I have many things to share, but their value is not in their content but in my offering of them and your acceptance – a dance, something which is alive and loving – Me! What I have to offer is ME.

I think that I was always interested in uncovering the mysteries of the universe. I think that as a child I somehow perceived the mystical nature of reality; perhaps this is something all children know. I marvel at how my life in its strange twists and turns has always brought me toward the discovery of the mystical, as if it only had one goal in mind. A recurring theme in my life has been the appreciation of small moments of magic. Small in 'consensus reality' terms, small in the eyes of the world and survival and the superego, but monumental in meaning. Each of these magical moments seemed to rip a window into the fabric of 'reality', offering a brief view beyond time and space into the heart of existence. And what do I see there? A level of reality where kindness, love and freedom are the very fabric of that reality.

Once, these moments were random and rare events. They seemed to come and go as they pleased. Although each one of these experiences filled me with wonder, their absence – often for years at a time – would leave me with a yearning that was hard to endure. To have been touched by the light and then to have lost it, without knowing how to get it back, felt like abandonment. Often it was easier to forget all about such things, to go on with life and all its demands, but deep down, forgetting was not possible. Most of the time I would search for the magic in art, in love, in friendship – anywhere I could, but it always seemed tantalizingly just around the next corner. The things I was searching for proved ever elusive. Too often, having attained my goals I would feel a terrible emptiness.

Working with the inner judge means having constant access to the magic of the moment – an access which is not always easy, and I'll admit that I don't choose it nearly as often as I could. But I know that it is present and available at all times, and that makes a huge difference to my life. I gain particular enjoyment from allowing space for meaning and authenticity to open up in my relationships with others. So often the doorway presents itself by noticing that something feels wrong and then identifying a superego attack as the cause of the discomfort. So often my judgments and expectations of myself or others lead me into a kind of trance in which I only see an imaginary representation of reality. Once I notice it I can see how two-dimensional and lifeless the representation really is. Stepping aside from the judgment allows the wondrous aliveness of reality to return to my awareness. I feel again my beauty and I perceive the beauty and wonder of the other. What joy! What freedom!

I am filled with bliss as I write, and certainly it is a great blessing to have learned and remembered how to find my wonderful magic nearer than I ever could have imagined, but the question raises itself: why not choose this bliss more often? In my case it is because there is usually a sense of danger involved. It is the fear of the unknown. When did I learn to be afraid of the unknown? I don't know. I suppose everything that we call society instills this fear in us all, and I've no doubt that it serves a purpose. Personally, my growing ability and willingness to be present is all about learning to embrace this danger, and to call it adventure!

I learn a lot about myself from my daughter. On a recent holiday I was able to see firsthand how important and valuable an adventurous life is. We were with a group of friends staying on the south coast of New South Wales. The coastline is very rugged, and the ocean notoriously treacherous. We spent a day swimming out to a rocky island separated from a headland by a reef. We had to paddle and swim past the reef and then climb out of the water onto the rocks, timing our exits with the swell of the ocean. The ocean was relatively calm and the distances not excessive, nonetheless a sense of excitement and danger filled the entire outing, and Charlotte, who is 10, kept saying, 'Dad, this is like a REAL adventure!' I knew what she meant. Her delight at the chance to have a 'real' adventure filled her whole being with energy and aliveness, and the dangers she overcame have had a lasting and positive effect on her self-esteem. The natural high of that one day's outing lasted weeks.

The experience of dropping 'knowing' and allowing the magic of the moment to open up is not fundamentally different from an adventure to an exciting island. Both can be filled with a sense of danger and adventure which, if allowed, can lead to an aliveness which fills our whole being. Of course peace and rest are needed too, but I have found that they come as pairs; true aliveness allows true rest and vice versa. It is ironic that a life spent trying to be safe and secure is not restful. It certainly has not been so for me; the greatest moments of peace and rest I have known were in the depths of the unknown.

I have not arrived anywhere; I have only been waking up, and the world around me seems pregnant with possibilities. Possibilities for connection and meaning and magic.

Mandir trained as a violin maker in Cremona, Italy. For some years now he has been studying self-inquiry, inner judge work and Essence with Avikal. In 2009 he completed the 'Who is in?' Awareness Intensive facilitator training and is presently studying holistic counseling and psychotherapy. He lives in Sydney where he also practices Aikido.

Appendix A

What Is Inquiry and How Do We Practice It?

What inquiry is

The word 'inquiry', as used in the spiritual tradition, comprises: search, quest, investigation, exploration. (Ramana Maharshi, founder of the Advaita – non-duality – tradition, is considered one of the fathers of the spiritual search through inquiry. In fact he used the question 'Who am I?' to know himself and awaken to true nature. In Zen tradition, the use of Koans is meant to help the student focus on particular aspects of their mind and recognize their attachment to concepts, prejudices, and interpretations of reality. Osho devotes a whole book to the fundamentals of inquiry and the different phases of the search: *The Search: Ten Bulls of Zen*.)

An essential meaning in this context, however, that needs to be clear is that inquiry is not simply analysis, nor is it restricted to the field of logical deduction. On the contrary, inquiry that is really effective will continually bring us into contact with the unknown, challenging our convictions and everything we think we know.

Inquiry is a dynamic movement that, if practiced with passion and love, can take us outside 'our comfort zone' to territories way beyond our expectations and open us to profound and immediate understandings that would not be possible using linear logic.

We have already heard about inquiry in Chapter 1, but this appendix provides a great more detail on:

- The four fundamental pillars of inquiry
- The technique of inquiry and how to apply it

194

- Communicating with oneself and others during the process of inquiry.

The pillars of inquiry

There are four pillars – four essential components – of effective inquiry that we need to bear in mind. Having these strongly present will reinforce our inquiry, giving it clarity and the capacity to penetrate all the obfuscations that might normally render our search clouded and uncertain.

Will/intention

First, and foremost, there must be within us the will to know the truth.

This will is like a flame and manifests in our 'intention' to see, hear and experience – in every possible way – the truth of a given situation. This intention can be revealed only if we are willing to tell ourselves the truth about ourselves, even if that truth is painful, unexpected, hard to comprehend or, even, contrary to everything we have always thought.

The fuel of that flame is a love of the truth and the acknowledgment of the need for truth in order to know ourselves.

If we do not have 'intention', our search will be lukewarm, without vitality and ready to give way. So instead of truly performing an inquiry, we may look for justifications and explanations that allow us to feel at ease and in control of the situation.

If we do have intention, the inquiry becomes a commitment to ourselves that supports and helps us penetrate the defenses and the habitual nature of our behaviors, and fills the search with passion and trust in ourselves. Intention is a sword that helps us to separate what is false and what isn't, allowing us to recognize any falsehood for what it is, and to see with such intensity that with practice, we are enabled to live our daily life with presence.

But it also does something else: it consciously reconnects us with our soul and the soul's yearning to know itself by connecting us with one of the fundamental drives for human evolution – curiosity.

Man is the only animal in existence who has freedom – and out of the freedom is agony. Agony means: I don't know who I am. I don't know where I'm going and why I am going. I don't know whether whatever I'm doing I am supposed to do or not... This is the agony – that the meaning is not known, that the purpose is not known, that the goal is not known... Existence has let man utterly free. Once you become aware of this situation then agony arises. And it is fortunate to feel it. That is why I say it is not ordinary pain, suffering, misery. It is very extraordinary, and it is of tremendous value to your whole life, its growth, that you should feel agony, that each fibre of your being should feel the questioning, that you should become simply a question.

(Osho, *From Darkness to Light*, The Rebel Publishing, Cologne, 1983, ch. 8)

Openness

The second essential component is 'openness' to what we encounter while practicing inquiry. When we explore a situation with intention, both internally and externally, activating our love for the truth, we will find things we are not aware of, that we have hidden and tried to avoid by repressing them in our unconscious. Usually, right at the beginning, we come into contact with our superego, its judgments and prejudices, our structures of defense, the usual mechanisms through which we sustain our personality, our inner images and the ways in which we try to control ourselves and our relationships. Opening ourselves to the unconscious is not a game. And it is not always pleasant.

Being open, then, means being willing to accept – totally and immediately – what appears in the present moment. This also means telling the truth as it is: I am angry, I am afraid, I would like to run away, I feel blocked, I don't know what to do, I'm in a state of shock, I feel lost, I am closed, and so on.

An awareness without choice or judgment, a direct and simple reflection of our experience, without trying to manipulate, to glamorize, to make palatable or acceptable. It means to also observe the tendency to judge and compare, and to see what effects it has on us and on others.

In 'The Guest House', a poem by Rumi, Persian poet of the 13th century, is a beautiful expression of this quality of 'openness'. (Rumi, *The Essential Rumi*, Translations by Coleman Barks, Harper San Francisco, 1995, p. 109)

This being human is a guest house.
Every morning a new arrival.
A joy, a depression, a meanness,
Some momentary awareness comes
As an unexpected visitor.
Welcome and entertain them all!
Even if they're a crowd of sorrows,
Who violently sweep your house
Empty of its furniture,
Still, treat each guest honorably.
He may be clearing you out
For some delight.
The dark thought, the shame, the malice,
Meet them at the door laughing,
And invite them in.
Be grateful for whoever comes,
Because each has been sent
As a guide from beyond.

Acknowledging not-knowing

The third pillar is 'acknowledging not knowing'. Acknowledging not-knowing means being aware that all our knowledge is the result of events that happened in the past, and that we cannot automatically apply that knowledge to what happens to us in the present. Certainly that knowledge is useful and can help us to read what happens but, at the same time, it can become an obstacle to our ability to answer – in a creative and original way – to events that happen 'here and now'. In fact, if we pay attention, we can see that most of our behaviors are reactions based on past experiences, and that this is one of the fundamental reasons for the sense of repetitiveness and imprisonment we feel.

The truth? This moment, and the next, and the next, are all unknown until they happen: the words that you read, the light around you, the sensations you have, the way you sit and breathe, the temperature of your body, the emotions that you feel and the thoughts that cross your mind, everything is new and has never happened before.

This is not difficult to understand and accept. The present is unknown until it happens. Whatever the reading is of this unknown moment through knowledge accumulated in the past, will inevitably be inadequate. We will be interpreting it through our heads, feelings... the existential experience of the present moment that is alive here and now, will be trapped inside conceptual categories basically of mental significance, based on memory and abstract evaluation. Living the present moment with an awareness of not knowing means to be open to whatever happens both inside and out, and to accept the events without a priori knowledge. It is vital to understand that not knowing is a living and flexible thing that responds in a spontaneous and organic way to what happens, without preconceived filters, refusal or exclusion.

The awareness of not knowing is, in its openness, curious, inclusive and sensitive; it is capable of accepting and doesn't need filters to interpret what happens even though they bring with them the illusion of controlling what happens.

Through this conscious attitude of not knowing, we can find our freedom from the superego; our attachment to our personal story begins to dissolve. The baggage of the past becomes lighter, little by little.

Do we have to throw away what we know? Certainly not! We simply recognize the limits of an interpretation of the present based only on that knowledge. And, when we do this, we are open to the revelation of the significance of the present experience that can only manifest when it is not obscured by a priori interpretations.

Socrates, declared the wisest man in Greece by the Delphic oracle, invited us to 'know thyself'. When his disciples asked him what he thought about being labeled the wisest man in Greece, the philosopher answered that he didn't understand how it was possible, since the only thing he was sure he knew was that he did not know. The disciples went to Delphi to ask the oracle why, then, was Socrates chosen as the wisest man. The oracle responded, 'It's for this reason I have chosen Socrates, because he is the only one who knows he doesn't know.'

One of the fundamental actions on any journey 'to know ourselves' is to let go of the attachment to what we think we know and to recognize how that knowledge restricts our ability to have a direct experience of the present moment. In fact, the knowledge that we carry with us becomes, with its baggage of concepts, judgments, prejudices, beliefs, an energetic, intellectual and emotional quantity that separates us from the moment and its totality. When we acknowledge not knowing, then we are able to be present in every experience that life presents us with.

Being with all that arises means that we allow ourselves to witness all that occurs with equanimity – even our own tendency to censor or shape experience. Whether angry, curious, or bored, immersed in an exciting flow of ideas or captivated by a story, we practice mindfulness. Gradually, a capacity for breadth of awareness and stillness at depth develops in us. Even as the surface of consciousness is roiled by waves, a deeper presence is quiet and aware. We sense streams of consciousness, care, and wisdom that are ordinarily hidden. We see not just a few trees but the whole forest, the branching network of roots beneath the forest, and the animals that call the forest home. Being with all that arises, we come into dynamic relationship with the intrinsic intelligence and endless creativity of life itself, manifest moment by moment through the unfolding of personal and collective experience. We learn to rest in the still point at the heart of activity and to sense the subtle movement in stillness.

(Thomas J. Hurley, *Archetypal Practices for Collective Wisdom*, Collective Wisdom Initiative, Seed Paper, 2004)

Staying in the body

The fourth pillar is 'staying in the body'. Our conditioning is not an idea or a concept; on the contrary, it is first of all a presence in the body. Conditioning means judgments, opinions, values, beliefs, prejudices at a psychological and emotional level, as well as at a physical level like a web of tensions, contractions, blocks, insensitivity, chronic postures and somatic illnesses.

Generally we try to avoid our tensions or to redress them as quickly as possible and the result (if there is one) is usually, temporary and limited. We have learnt to treat our body as something we live in and with which we have to reckon. As if it is something at a lower level, down there! Our moral and religious prejudices lead us to treat our body with little attention or affection, if not with disgust and hate.

And yet it is our body, more than any other part of ourselves, that allows us to experience life. Our senses are the doors of our perception and without them how would we exist? To be present in the 'here and now' and do inquiry we need to be able to stay in our body and feel how thoughts and emotions are linked to precise physical sensations. This ability to stay in our body will give us roots and a sense of depth and solidity to experiences that might be too evanescent and too fleeting to grasp. Recognizing, at a physical level, the symptoms associated with certain judgments linked to the superego's attacks, and of the emotional load and associated defenses, allows us to unify all levels of our consciousness: physical, mental and emotional, and to accurately identify the pattern of a particular behavior.

It firmly establishes our spiritual growth in the physicality of the experience. The body is here and now; it is down to earth. The mind and the emotions are hardly ever in the here and now. They live mostly in the past and the future as children of memory and of desire. The body is here: it feels, it sees, it perceives.

Consider particular physical sensations, now, in the light of what we know about inquiry. The tightness one feels in the chest is not separated from the sadness one feels nor from the memory of a wound received or from the desire to heal and recover from a painful episode.

To recognize and understand the event that caused the pain, to connect with the emotion and express it, is fundamental; but not enough, if I don't come to terms with the energetic contraction that keeps blocking the breath in my chest.

Instead of trying to free my body of the recurring symptoms, I can learn to experience the presence and to be here, to keep my attention on a particular part of my body and a sensation, or a series of sensations, and to use them like a door in my unconscious.

How to practice inquiry

Inquiry can be practiced at many levels. The appropriate level depends on the object we choose for the inquiry and the ability we have developed to focus our attention on the experience while it happens. The most immediate level and closer to us (and the one we confine ourselves to in these pages) is concerned with how our personality functions and with our personal history. In this ambit we could, for example, choose to explore a question related to a particular episode from our childhood, or to a current relationship with a friend or a child, or the relationship we have with success or money, or the question of jealousy and its presence in our daily life, and so on.

The choice of object can be very precise or more general. For example, in Chapter 2 we ask: 'What was the atmosphere like in your family when you were a child? What memories do you have of that atmosphere and of yourself in it? How did you feel? What was the environment like where you grew up? Were your parents present in your life? Did you have any physical contact with them, or one of them? What kind? Did you feel supported and recognized, or not? What was appreciated, supported, what were the things considered of value and what was condemned, rejected or hidden?'

This is quite a general question and aims to activate some memories and the emotions associated with it. When you practice inquiry, the first thing that you can explore is 'the story' – what you already know; the information you remember and in some way have already worked through and perhaps digested, and your evaluations and thoughts about particular events.

This first stage of inquiry is related to the past and to your accumulated knowledge. To do this you could describe some episodes that come to the surface and for example, talk about the fact that in your family everything to do with sex was taboo, and mention episodes where your curiosity about sex caused you to be humiliated or punished. You might want to talk about the way cultural and intellectual pursuits were absolutely supported at the expense of play and fun and how all this created an atmosphere of seriousness, or you can talk about other episodes that concerned you. This first part of inquiry, then, concerns your personal history; we use it to 'open the box'.

Subsequently, you can begin to observe the effects the telling of that story produces in your body in this moment. Bringing your attention to the body and what happens in it, the story then is seen in its current existence. For example, you might notice that the solar plexus contracts and you experience a difficulty in breathing, as well as a general sense of heaviness. When you observe all this and widen your attention to include the presence of emotions, you might also notice that you are sad and that together with that sadness there's a sense of frustration, and that the first one is related to the heaviness while the second one is related to the tension in the solar plexus.

This second phase of the exploration brings you into the present, binding the memory and related emotions to the effects they have on your body, in the present. What is, in fact, happening is that the tensions or other sensations associated with particular events come to awareness when we direct our attention, and this allows us to begin singling out a web of correlations that includes thoughts, emotions, physical sensations, the involvement of the superego, defenses, and so on. Often we feel we are finding the pieces of a puzzle and we begin to see how they might fit into each other.

The history, and the knowledge related to it, functions as information that gives us the direction for the research. When we open our consciousness to the present moment, becoming aware of our physical sensations and emotional feelings, we begin to enter the unknown that is manifesting.

If we don't rush to find a definition and explanation but let the thread of awareness join the pieces of the puzzle in its own time, then, and only then, will the meaning of the experience begin to reveal itself and the picture begin to emerge. The 'knowing that we don't know' works as a glue that joins the significant pieces beyond linear logic, acting in all directions at the same time and aligning mind, body, emotions and soul.

> This is the nature of revelation: it is a process of the creation and destruction of knowledge because not-knowing is the ground from which knowledge arises ... Not-knowing is the entry to the adventure of discovery. In time, you may recognize that not-knowing is the way Being opens up to its own mysteriousness. In fact, this not-knowing is the direct expression of the Mystery itself ... Mystery is the essence of Being itself, which manifests in inquiry as an openness that appears as not-knowing ... every time that we recognize that we don't know, a new kind of knowledge is revealed.
>
> (A. H. Almaas, *Spacecruiser Inquiry*, Shambhala Publications, Boston, 2002, pp. 102, 103.)

The steps to take: Summing up

Performing the inquiry will be very effective if you:

- Formulate a question concerning the object of your inquiry that gives a general direction of where you want to go
- Tell the story: what you already know in regard to that subject
- Widen your attention and notice the effects that this recounting has on you in the present, including the sensations in your body, emotions and images as they appear in your consciousness
- Observe if the superego is active, whether it attacks you, if there are judgments or symptoms of inner conflict.

Don't draw quick conclusions: activate your curiosity and continue to formulate questions about what is happening; the reason for certain symptoms, the relations with certain emotions, what is behind a particular defense, what the superego's judgments remind you of. Maintain the contact with the thread while it unravels (even if it appears fragmented).

How to communicate with yourself and with others

Another aspect of inquiry that is very powerful and will add intensity to your research is to use communication – either with yourself, consciously, or with others.

If you decide to practice inquiry on your own, you have three ways to communicate: writing, speaking, or a combination of both. Each way has benefits and can produce results. The simplest way to start might be to write and regularly keep track of the development of the research. Writing helps you to formulate the experience in a slower and more precise way than simply making internal cerebral observations. Writing involves your body and the need to articulate, and it also encourages you to be precise in your thinking, in your choice of words. However, writing can be a distraction from the experience itself because it forces us to mediate through writing.

Speaking can also be a powerful tool. The great advantage of speaking aloud is the element of sound; that saying some words and hearing them said brings them to consciousness faster. The easiest way to communicate when you are alone is in a loud voice in front of a mirror or a wall, as if you were facing another person.

Even more powerful, but also more difficult for a lot of people, is to talk to another person who offers to listen – and only to listen. In this case you have to clearly ask the person listening to you, to avoid commenting on what you are communicating (we don't want another superego in front of us) and to ask for explanations at the end of the communication only if the person communicating is fine with such dissection.

If you are working with another person, be sure to fix a time limit for the exploration. Generally 15–20 minutes for each inquiry question is feasible, but you can extend the time as you please. I advise you not to do more than 40 minutes, or if you are committed to doing longer sessions, at least take a break every 40 minutes.

The third method involves spoken and written communication, in a combination of the ways already described. Writing can be used at the beginning of the inquiry session in order to open a particular question by stimulating your knowledge of the subject in question, or at the end, to sum up the experience and join the pieces, or you can do it in both ways. If you practice inquiry with someone else, a good way is to do 20–30 minutes per person.

Laura's story

What follows is the process of inquiry of one of my students. I decided to put it here as it includes many of the elements just mentioned before. You will find a very alive curiosity supported and energized by a clear will to understand and know the truth. You will find an acute attention to how the experience unfolds through physical sensations and how these are often associated with a particular emotion. You will also notice how experiences of expansion and contraction coexist. And you will find a readiness to accept what is there and a flexibility and letting go of fixed notions about one's self. You will also find how new meaning is revealed step after step as the result of the process of inquiry.

Laura is about 35 years of age. She is a brilliant violinist, quite well known, and the mother of a four-year-old girl. For some years she has been involved in spiritual search and for the last two, in particular, she has been working on her superego. Part of her personal development has been directed at discovering how she can help herself and other young artists to play music with more joy, in an original way, and with less anxiety and pressure. What follows is her journey of exploration.

'I am lying on my bed after a very restless night. I am aware of a familiar sensation: I don't feel completely rested.

There is tension in my jaw and back, and it prevents me from going back to sleep. I begin to observe where the tension seems to be strongest, the jaw, and I remember how I resist my vulnerability clenching the mouth. Suddenly I see my face like a mask of stern discipline, the same as an army general would have. There is a voice that says, "You will do it my way; there is no other way than mine." I feel confused because I don't have any idea of what this way is. There is an order but no help or advice. I remember my father, and my mother. I reflect on the fact that neither of them had ever said these things openly. My mother was the one who insisted that I do things as she wanted. The jaw relaxes slightly. Underneath there is a sensation of fear that says: "I don't know who I am, if I don't do it my way." There is the fear that if I lose this sense of discipline I will lose the respect of others that is so important to me. I feel the horror of my father towards those who don't play the career game. That horror, the mistrust, the fear are also in me. There is a distinct fear of becoming completely useless and full of shame, of not deserving my place in society.

I let this sense of uselessness be present and it seems to occupy a large and shapeless space. As I let myself feel that spaciousness it arises as a feeling that my personality cannot attach itself to anything in particular and this brings me further into the present. A sense of freedom is born from the feeling that I could do everything I want. I start laughing and being pervaded by a subtle joy. Even in all of this I notice that my superego is still trying to attack me and I feel the anxiety that the old structures of tension and effort that are in me are too strong, and I might be incapable of truly changing them. A voice inside says, "You tried often and for a long time to resolve this but you know you can't do it." I note that the attack from the superego tries to misrepresent my experience and to convince me that the change can only come through rigid discipline and effort. I do not engage in an inner dialogue with it.

Twenty minutes later, I am still in the present, joyful and in harmony with my daughter. There is the feeling that I have ample time and space to do what is required and to be with her.

Later that day, during a meditation, I ask for help to learn to relax and to let go of that military discipline. I am aware of the voice of my father who orders me not to be still. I feel the need for a good "Go to hell!" to be said to that voice inside. After which I become still and peaceful. I feel big and black like space, but completely in my body, with a red light around me as if a wild energy surrounded my body. I realize that I am the stillness, that it's impossible not to be stillness. I stay like this for a while and slowly I am conscious of myself and my energy. Then I feel my body lightly fold in on itself in shame. I feel that this shame is directly linked to that of my father. There is a miserable sorryness for the fact I exist. The message I feel inside is: "You should not exist!" I see my father's hermit existence in a new light: he tried to disappear, and I can recognize this tendency in my life. As was the case when I felt the stillness, I now feel I exist, in a way that simply is. The quality of this sensation is incredibly gentle. I can nearly hear the sound of water running softly and there is a light frothy quality, with a soft blue light. The reassuring sensation is that my existence cannot hurt because it is more harmonious, inviting and impeccably capable of sustaining me than I had ever imagined.

The following day, I am playing Bach on my violin. It's going well... the thought comes to me that I should finally make a record. But I let it go and at that point I am aware of my mind being very preoccupied. The superego is saying to me, "Your mind should not be empty while you play!" It seems that my parents and other adults, all want this for me: this intuition leads to a pause appearing, gaps in the chattering, and reveals a vast silence that listens to me playing. I move my attention to this observer and from this detached space I notice how convinced I usually am that I should be emotionally involved while playing. That I should actually burst with emotion. The superego tells me all the time that to hold the public I have to penetrate their space with my emotions or I won't be able to reach them.

After noticing all this I start to play freely from my own space. From this space it seems irrelevant if they listen to me or not. I have all the space I need and this is all that counts. An intuition from the preceding day comes to mind: that my energy will find its own way to meet the others, guided by its own harmonious intelligence. This understanding brings more relaxed feelings, moving me further away from the belief that I have to form and control my relationship with the public.'

Appendix B

Centering and Grounding

In many traditions – Chinese traditional medicine, martial arts, meditation – there is a fundamental principle that helps us to be more present, aware of our body and able to direct our energy. The principle states that attention guides awareness and awareness guides energy. This means that by learning to direct our attention where we desire, our awareness will follow and, with it, our energy. It also means that if we want to move or shift our energy we can do it by moving our attention.

Most of the people I have worked with, in my groups or in individual sessions, sooner or later notice that in direct correspondence with the judge's attack there is something like a sudden loss of energy in the belly, a loss of feeling in the legs or in the lower part of the body, as if the body had disappeared from the hips down.

This feeling is very common but most of us are so used to it, we don't pay attention to it anymore; there is only a vague perception of overload in the head and of emptiness in the belly, in the genitals and in the legs, often together with a tension that separates the upper part from the lower. Generally this imbalance intensifies when the person is under attack from the judge. *(Wilhelm Reich has written in depth on emotional armor and different belts of tension that divide the body in parts.)*

Please note the exercises of respiration and meditation in this Appendix are intended to bring our attention to the belly and, in particular, to three points:

  a. the solar plexus: roughly three fingers below the sternum
  b. the *Tanden*: a Japanese term used in martial arts to indicate

a place about three fingers below the navel, inside the belly

c. the perineum: a point in the pelvic floor between the anus and the sexual organs.

These three points are connected to the presence and manifestation of our will, essential to our survival and associated issues, and to our intrinsic value.

When centering and grounding, we create the conditions for ourselves to be effective in the inquiry. This process allows us to more fully activate the sessions. Centering and grounding involves:

1. Shifting your attention from the external to the internal (making yourself, rather than the other, the center of your attention)
2. Moving your attention from the head to the belly (reconnecting and activating the other fundamental energy centers – the heart as the center of feelings; the belly as the instinctual center)
3. Reversing the energetic movement that, because of excessive mental activity, tends to accumulate in the head, and directing it towards the belly or the feet in harmony with the force of gravity
4. Slowing down the rhythm of the breath through abdominal respiration (instead of pectoral), facilitating relaxation
5. Revitalizing the belly and the lower part of the body, giving it your attention, awareness and energy.

The most immediate effects of centering and grounding will be a general feeling of expansion in sensorial awareness involving a clearer perception of ourselves and the external reality, a sense of density and solidity both physical and emotional, a feeling of connection between the upper and the lower parts of our body, a definite sense of easiness – often perceived in the beginning as lack of stress and preoccupation.

Meditations and visualizations

Meditations can be practiced sitting, standing, lying on your back or while moving. An essential part of the following practices is your being alert to the presence of the superego and the judgments that it makes about the way you do the exercises, about how you are, and so on. Visualizations – also called guided imagery – are an integral part of some meditations and are used mainly to support relaxation through inner images that we associate with serenity and flow like:

'See yourself as a cloud... floating... getting lighter and lighter...' or 'See yourself as a leaf in a gentle river as it flows down between the banks... not getting attached to anything in particular... free... unconcerned...' which are often used in hypnosis and NLP (Neuro Linguistic Programming).

Shift the attention with the breath

In a relaxed, seated position, close your eyes. Observe the way your attention moves from one thing to another. But don't make any effort to change what happens; simply be aware of your attention as it shifts from intense thought to light, fleeting thought, from one item to another, to a memory, to a physical sensation, to an emotion, to a noise, and so on. Let go of any effort to control the shifting of attention.

After a few minutes (2–3), put your hands on your belly below the navel. (You could, as an alternative, put your hands on the solar plexus or on the perineum. All three variations are useful.) Place one hand on top of the other, without pressing, and start to observe how you are breathing and the movement of your body while breathing. Observe the movement of your chest and shoulders, the sensations in your nose, in your chest and in your belly.

Slowly, without straining, let your breath go deeper, moving your belly. When you breathe in, the belly expands and when you breathe out the belly contracts, and the diaphragm goes down and up. Imagine your belly filling while breathing in, and emptying when breathing out. Every time you realize that your attention is wandering from this breathing practice (into the future or into the past), bring it back to the feelings in your hands and to the contact between the belly and the hands.

This practice will help you to relax and learn to be present with what is happening in the moment. The breath, as it happens in the now, works like an anchor of your focus. This capacity to focus will in time sharpen your attention both in terms of concentration as well as in terms of the capacity to be aware of multiple inputs at the same time.

The drop

This practice is a guided visualization and should be done sitting or standing.

Close your eyes and let your attention move freely. Place your hands one on top of the other over your belly. Little by little, bring your attention to the feelings in your hands and to the contact between the belly and hands, and go back to that contact every time you notice your mind is in the future or in the past. Relax the breath. Do not force yourself to direct it in any way.

Visualize a drop hanging in the center of your skull: a bright and shining drop, well defined against a dark backdrop, suspended in the center of your skull. Now you see it falling through the upper body: through the head, the throat, the chest, the stomach and into a pool of water filling your belly. Watch the ripples as it reaches the water: concentric circles that widen. Go back to, and visualize another drop and let it fall, and follow the previous procedure. Proceed like this for a few minutes (8–10), and when the last drop falls, rest your attention on the pool that fills your belly. After a couple of minutes lie on your back and don't do anything. Just rest.

The spiral

The purpose of this exercise is to gather the energy in the lower belly particularly in the Tanden (three fingers below the navel, inside the belly). This point is considered the natural storeroom of energy in the body and in Zen, in martial arts, in Chinese medicine and in other teachings, is also considered the spiritual center of Being. It's also very close to the body's center of gravity.

Sit cross-legged on a pillow that lifts your buttocks slightly, stretch your spine, imagining that there is a thread tied to the back of your head that pulls from the top, and you are hanging like a puppet. It's a light stretching – don't strain yourself – but try to keep the backbone straight and the head straight on the shoulders too.

Relax the jaw and let the mouth open slightly as if, with a breath, you are saying 'Ahh' and, if possible, keep the mouth relaxed during the exercise. The exercise takes at least 10 minutes. Once you become familiar with the technique you can practice for up to 20 minutes, if you want.

Relax the shoulders, raising them during the inhalation and letting them fall during the exhalation. Do this 3 or 4 times.

The spiral is a form into which you will bend your body. Begin by bending the upper part of the body to the right, moving it forward, then to the left, then back and again to the right and continue this circular movement.

If you imagine sitting on the face of a large clock, the movement is anticlockwise (if you do this exercise below the equator you have to change the direction of the rotation and make it clockwise). The spine remains as straight as possible and the head is in line with the backbone, forming the axis of an inverted cone with its point being the perineum.

You will need to find a reasonably smooth rhythm for your movement – not too slow. A good way to find the rhythm is to count from 1 to 10 for the whole rotation, from the moment you bend to the side until you return to the starting position. Maintaining awareness of the speed of the movement and position of the body is vital: you will notice that as soon as you start thinking of something unrelated to what you are doing, you'll lose the rhythm and the spine will no longer be straight and the mouth will close, and so on.

Focus on the body! This spiraling movement collects the energy in the Tanden. After about 10 minutes start to slow down the movement until you finally come to a halt. Keep your focus on the Tanden and if you need help to do this, place your hands one on top of the other over the lower belly. After a few minutes, lie on your back and rest for a while.

At the end of this meditation you will most often experience a very alive flow of energy all over your body and a general sense of regeneration. You will also be more aware of the lower part of your body and possibly feel it heavier and more compact. This often brings a sense of inner support and solidity. It's a great technique to practice when you feel unsettled, unclear, very emotional or too busy in your head.

The spiraling movement in fact, through collecting most of the energy in the Tanden, will clear your mind and unload stress. It might also give you a sense of strength and presence.

Stop!

This exercise can be done during the day, and it can be done often. In fact, the more you do it the better it is. Tradition says it should be done at least 7 times a day. This practice is about giving yourself the time to stop! And to stop completely, sitting or walking, at your desk, in the bus, while cooking, wherever you can, for 30 to 60 seconds. If possible, close your eyes, though you can do it with your eyes open, even if it is more difficult at the beginning.

Turn all your attention inside and simply notice your

thoughts, the sensations in the body, whether there are emotions. Let go of what is happening outside and concentrate on what's happening inside; be aware of the way you breathe, if there are any tensions, the heartbeat, the sensations in the skin, if you are calm or not, how you are feeling. Are you content, sad, worried, happy, feeling alive? Observe yourself carefully and with acceptance for 30 seconds without changing anything. Notice if your judge is present and if it tells you how you should be.

By consciously creating gaps through the Stop, you will start noticing that what appears to be a continuous flow of thoughts, emotions and sensations is in fact not a continuum and that there is space between thoughts and emotions and sensations.

In fact they are just objects of your awareness. Non-material objects, but objects still.

And they exist in space as every object like a chair, or this book, or your body. By practicing 'Stop!' you might start noticing that there is actually lots of space. As in the physical world in fact, space is what is present the most. Just look around and notice right now how space is the necessary condition for you being able to perceive all the physical objects around you. In the same way, in the inner world, space is the necessary condition for you to be able to perceive thoughts, emotions and sensations.

The more you will become aware of the presence of space, the more you will be able to relax and slow down.

Open your eyes like two windows

The eyes have a direct connection with your Tanden. When the eyes and the gaze are tense our attention tends to 'go out' and we lose our connection with the belly. Try to do this exercise standing with at least 3 or 4 meters of space in front of you.

To begin, close your eyes, and relax your knees (let them bend slightly) and then bring your attention to the soles of your feet. Feel how the weight falls on the feet; notice whether there is more weight at the front or on the side or on the back parts of your feet, and slowly bring the weight to a point in the center so that the weight falls on all of the sole.

Imagine your feet are like the roots of a tree and feel how the floor is supporting you. Relax your buttocks and your shoulders; let the breath become slower and deeper. After some minutes, open your eyes and look straight ahead while continuing to keep your attention on the soles of your feet. Now let your gaze relax. You can achieve this by not fixing your eyes on a particular object, but rather by embracing everything in front of you with your gaze. It's like putting your vision slightly out of focus. An image that portrays this, and is often helpful, is that of two windows opening onto reality and letting in all that there is, without choosing, without judgment, without preferences. You simply see.

Stay like this for 2 to 3 minutes then close your eyes and, placing your hands one on top of the other over the belly, shift your attention to the Tanden. After a couple of minutes repeat the exercise.

It seems that we lose nearly 70% of our energy through the eyes and the effort of focusing. This effort contributes to a very spread sense of heaviness in the ocular segment and to headaches and migraines. This efforting also generates tensions in the back of the skull, in the neck and in the shoulders and it is connected emotionally with the need to control and a basic mistrust about what surrounds us. As you start relaxing your eyes, the associated tensions will begin to fade and the visual perception will become softer and gentler and, paradoxically, also sharper and with more depth.

Learn to listen

This exercise is very much like the previous one but instead of opening the eyes and looking, you keep them closed and shift your attention completely to your hearing. Create the same stance as you did for Stop. Imagine your feet are like the roots of a tree and feel how the floor is supporting you. Relax your buttocks and your shoulders; let the breath become slower and deeper. After some minutes, open your eyes and look straight ahead while continuing to keep your attention on the soles of your feet. Listen to the sounds around you. Again, open your hearing and don't choose what you hear; let the sounds reach you.

After a while, listen to the sound of the breath inside you. If possible, keep your attention on the inside and outside at the same time. Notice what kind of sensations you feel when you hear without seeing. Observe whether you are able to listen without immediately labeling what you hear. After some minutes, lie down and rest.

These exercises are useful by themselves to support presence, to help relaxing, to become aware of places of stress and tension, and, in general, to be more in touch with what is happening to you in the moment. You can practice them every time it seems appropriate, especially when you find yourself in emotional whirlwinds, in moments of confusion or worry, or when you simply want to feel centered and in contact with the earth and yourself.

At the same time these exercises are a notable support in learning to defend oneself from the superego. A very good learning ground is to be aware of how the superego attacks you because you don't practice the exercises properly, or with enough attention or by saying that you could do them better.

Don't listen; do the exercises and continue to do them until they become familiar and you can do them without instructions.

As you become familiar with the techniques, you might start noticing how they affect you and possibly find what helps you the most depending on different situations.

Start by experimenting with one at a time for a week-long period and possibly take some notes on effects, insights, difficulties, results.

These techniques do not have a particular time of the day associated, as some other meditations do, so feel free to experiment at different times.

If you find one in particular to be your favorite then start using it regularly.

Bibliography

Almaas, A. H.
Facets of Unity, Diamond Books, Berkeley 1998
Work on the Superego, Diamond Books, Berkeley 1992
The Elixir of Enlightenment, Samuel Weiser, York Beach 1998
The Point of Existence, Diamond Books, Berkeley 1996
Spacecruiser Inquiry, Shambhala Publications, Boston 2002
Brown, Byron
Soul without Shame, Shambhala Publications, Boston 1999
Costantino, Avikal E.
Tackling the Medusa Within, Viha Connection, Mill Valley,
March/April 2004
Davis, John
The Diamond Approach, Shambhala Publications, Boston 1999
Hurley, Thomas J.
Archetypal Practices for Collective Wisdom, Collective Wisdom
Initiative, Seed Paper 2004
Kimura, Yasuhiko Genku
Project Beauty and Freedom from Fear and Guilt, VIA, vol. 2, no.
3/4, USA 2004
Maitri, Sandra
The Spiritual Dimension of the Enneagram, Tarcher & Putnam,
New York 2000
Marx, Karl
Critique of the Gotha Program, Penguin Classics
Osho
Unio Mystica, Rajneesh Foundation, Pune 1980
The Discipline of Transcendence, Rajneesh Foundation, Pune 1978
My Way: The Way of the White Clouds, Rajneesh Foundation,
Pune 1977
Zen: The Path of Paradox, Rajneesh Foundation, Pune 1978
The Search, Rajneesh Foundation, Pune 1977

From Darkness to Light, The Rebel Publishing, Cologne 1983
Nowhere To Go But In, Chapter 13, online library,
www.osho.com
Rumi
The Essential Rumi, Translations by Coleman Barks, Harper, San
Francisco 1995

Acknowledgments

This book is the result of many years of search for the truth. In this time I had the fortune to meet masters and teachers who helped me recognize the luminosity and intelligence of my soul. Two in particular have deeply touched my life: Osho and Faisal Muqaddam.

I am also very grateful to all the friends that have contributed to this book with their life and work experiences. And finally I want to thank Amira, my companion, for being with me in this journey that we enjoy immensely.

Avikal E. Costantino is a spiritual teacher. Curiosity, passion and love for the truth guide his teaching and are conveyed clearly and penetratingly. He is founder and director of the Integral Being Institute which is active in Europe, Asia and Australia. He lives in Sydney.

www.integralbeing.com
www.avikal.net

BOOKS